THE WORKS OF JAMES WHITCOMB RILEY ✤ ✤
VOL. IX

THE POEMS AND PROSE
❧ ❧ SKETCHES OF ❧ ❧
JAMES WHITCOMB RILEY

ARMAZINDY

CHARLES SCRIBNER'S
SONS ❧ NEW YORK ❧ 1908

Copyright, 1894, 1898, by
JAMES WHITCOMB RILEY

---

*_** *The publication of this volume in the Homestead Edition of the works of James Whitcomb Riley is made possible by the courtesy of The Bowen-Merrill Company, of Indianapolis, the original publishers of Mr. Riley's books.*

TO

HENRY EITEL

CONTENTS

ARMAZINDY

Armazindy	3
The Old Trundle-Bed	15
Natural Perversities	17
The Old School-Chum	20
Writin' Back to the Home-Folks	22
The Blind Girl	25
We Defer Things	28
The Muskingum Valley	29
For this Christmas	31
A Poor Man's Wealth	32
The Little Red Ribbon	34
"How did You Rest, Last Night?"	35
A Good-Bye	37
When Maimie Married	38
"This Dear Child-Hearted Woman that is Dead"	40
To a Poet-Critic	41
An Old-Timer	42
The Silent Victors	44
Up and Down Old Brandywine	51

CONTENTS

	PAGE
THREE SINGING FRIENDS	56
A NOON LULL	59
A WINDY DAY	60
MY HENRY	62
THE SONG I NEVER SING	64
TO EDGAR WILSON NYE	67
LITTLE DAVID	68
OUT OF THE HITHERWHERE	69
RABBIT IN THE CROSS-TIES	71
SERENADE—TO NORA	72
THE LITTLE WHITE HEARSE	74
WHAT REDRESS	76
DREAMER, SAY	77
WHEN LIDE MARRIED *HIM*	79
MY BRIDE THAT IS TO BE	81
"RINGWORM FRANK"	85
AN EMPTY GLOVE	87
OUR OWN	89

MAKE-BELIEVE AND CHILD-PLAY

The Frog	93
"TWIGGS AND TUDENS"	95
DOLORES	113
WHEN I DO MOCK	114
MY MARY	115
Eros	118
ORLIE WILDE	119
LEONAINIE	128
TO A JILTED SWAIN	130

CONTENTS

	PAGE
THE VOICES	131
A Barefoot Boy	134
THE YOUTHFUL PATRIOT	135
PONCHUS PILUT	136
A TWINTORETTE	139
SLUMBER-SONG	140
THE CIRCUS PARADE	141
FOLKS AT LONESOMEVILLE	143
THE THREE JOLLY HUNTERS	144
THE LITTLE DOG-WOGGY	146
CHARMS	148
A FEW OF THE BIRD-FAMILY	150
THROUGH SLEEPY-LAND	151
THE TRESTLE AND THE BUCK-SAW	153
THE KING OF OO-RINKTUM-JING	154
THE TOY PENNY-DOG	156
JARGON-JINGLE	157
THE GREAT EXPLORER	158
THE SCHOOL-BOY'S FAVORITE	159
ALBUMANIA	162
THE LITTLE MOCK-MAN	165
SUMMER-TIME AND WINTER-TIME	168
HOME-MADE RIDDLES	169
THE LOVELY CHILD	171
THE YELLOWBIRD	172
ENVOY	173

ARMAZINDY

ARMAZINDY

ARMAZINDY;—fambily name
Ballenger,—you'll find the same,
As her Daddy answered it,
In the old War-rickords yit,—
And, like him, she's airnt the good
Will o' all the neighberhood.—
Name ain't down in *History*,—
But, i jucks! it *ort* to be!
Folks is got respec' fer *her*—
Armazindy Ballenger!—
'Specially the ones 'at knows
Fac's o' how her story goes
From the start:—Her father blowed
Up—eternally furloughed—
When the old "Sultana" bu'st,
And sich men wuz needed wusst.—
Armazindy, 'bout fourteen-
Year-old then—and thin and lean

ARMAZINDY

As a killdee,—but—*my la!*—
Blamedest nerve you ever saw!
The girl's mother'd *allus* be'n
Sickly—wuz consumpted when
Word came 'bout her husband.—So
Folks perdicted *she'd* soon go—
(Kind o' grief *I* understand,
Losin' *my* companion,—and
Still a widower—and still
Hinted at, like neighbors will!)
So, app'inted, as folks said,
Ballenger a-bein' dead,
Widder, 'peared-like, gradjully,
Jes grieved after him tel *she*
Died, nex' Aprile wuz a year,—
And in Armazindy's keer
Leavin' the two twins, as well
As her pore old miz'able
Old-maid aunty 'at had be'n
Struck with palsy, and wuz then
Jes a he'pless charge on *her*—
Armazindy Ballenger.

Jevver watch a primrose 'bout
Minute 'fore it blossoms out—

ARMAZINDY

Kindo' loosen-like, and blow
Up its muscles, don't you know,
And, all suddent, bu'st and bloom
Out life-size?—Well, I persume
'At's the only measure I
Kin size Armazindy by!—
Jes a *child, one* minute,—nex',
Woman-grown, in all respec's
And intents and purposuz—
'At's what Armazindy wuz!

Jes a *child*, I tell ye! Yit
She made things git up and git
Round that little farm o' hern!—
Shouldered all the whole concern;—
Feed the stock, and milk the cows—
Run the *farm* and run the *house!*—
Only thing she didn't do
Wuz to plough and harvest too—
But the house and childern took
Lots o' keer—and had to look
After her old fittified
Grandaunt.—Lord! ye could 'a' cried,
Seein' Armazindy smile,
'Peared-like, sweeter all the while!

ARMAZINDY

And I've heerd her laugh and say:—
"Jes afore Pap marched away,
He says, 'I depend on *you*,
Armazindy, come what may—
You must be a Soldier, too!'"

Neighbers, from the fust, 'ud come—
And she'd *let* 'em help her *some*,—
"Thanky, ma'am!" and "Thanky, sir!"
But no charity fer *her!*—
"*She* could raise the means to pay
Fer her farm-hands ever' day
Sich wuz needed!"—And she *could*—
In cash-money jes as good
As farm-produc's ever brung
Their perducer, *old* er young!
So folks humored her and smiled,
And at last wuz rickonciled
Fer to let her have her own
Way about it.—But a-goin'
Past to town, they'd stop and see
"Armazindy's fambily,"
As they'd allus laugh and say,
And look sorry right away,
Thinkin' of her Pap, and how
He'd indorse his "Soldier" now!

ARMAZINDY

'Course *she* couldn't never be
Much in *young-folks'* company—
Plenty of *in*-vites to go,
But das't leave the house, you know—
'Less'n *Sund'ys* sometimes, when
Some old *Granny* 'd come and 'ten'
Things, while Armazindy *has*
Got away fer Church er " Class."
Most the youngsters *liked* her—and
'Twuzn't hard to understand,—
Fer, by time she wuz sixteen,
Purtier girl you never seen—
'Ceptin' she lacked schoolin', ner
Couldn't rag out stylisher—
Like some *neighber*-girls, ner thumb
On their blame' melodium,
Whilse their pore old mothers sloshed
Round the old back-porch and washed
Their clothes fer 'em—rubbed and scrubbed
Fer girls'd ort to jes be'n clubbed!

—And jes sich a girl wuz Jule
Reddinhouse.—*She'd* be'n to school
At *New Thessaly*, i gum!—
Fool before, but that he'pped *some*—

ARMAZINDY

'Stablished-like more confidence
'At she *never* had no sense.
But she wuz a cunnin', sly,
Meek and lowly sort o' lie,
'At men-folks like me and you
B'lieves jes 'cause we ortn't to.—
Jes as purty as a snake,
And as *pizen*—mercy sake!
Well, about them times it wuz,
Young Sol Stephens th'ashed fer us;
And we sent him over to
Armazindy's place to do
Her work fer her.—And-sir!   Well—
Mighty little else to tell,—
Sol he fell in love with her—
Armazindy Ballenger!

Bless ye!—'Ll, of all the love
'At I've ever yit knowed of,
That-air case o' theirn beat all!
W'y, she *worshipped* him!—And Sol,
'Peared-like, could 'a' kissed the sod
(Sayin' is) where that girl trod!
Went to town, she did, and bought
Lot o' things 'at neighbers thought

ARMAZINDY

Mighty strange fer *her* to buy,—
Raal chintz dress-goods—and 'way high!—
Cut long in the skyrt,—also
Gaiter-pair o' shoes, you know;
And lace collar;—yes, and fine
Stylish hat, with ivy-vine
And red ribbons, and these-'ere
Artificial flowers and queer
Little beads and spangles, and
Oysturch-feathers round the band!
Wore 'em, Sund'ys, fer a while—
Kindo' went to Church in style,
Sol and Armazindy!—Tel
It was noised round purty well
They wuz *promised.*—And they wuz—
Sich news travels—well it does!—
Pity 'at *that* did!—Fer jes
That-air fac' and nothin' less
Must 'a' putt it in the mind
O' Jule Reddinhouse to find
Out some dratted way to hatch
Out *some* plan to break the match—
'Cause she *done* it!—*How?* they's **none**
Knows adzac'ly *what* she done;
Some claims she writ letters to
Sol's folks, up nigh Pleasant View

ARMAZINDY

Somers—and described, you see,
"Armazindy's fambily"—
Hintin' "ef Sol married *her*,
He'd jes be pervidin' fer
Them-air twins o' hern, and old
Palsied aunt 'at couldn't hold
Spoon to mouth, and layin' near
Bedrid' on to eighteen year',
And still likely, 'pearantly,
To live out the century!"
Well—whatever plan Jule laid
Out to reach the p'int she made,
It wuz *desper't*.—And she won,
Finully, by marryun
Sol herse'f—*e-lopin'*, too,
With him, like she *had* to do,—
'Cause her folks 'ud allus swore
"Jule should never marry pore!"

This-here part the story I
Allus haf to hurry by,—
Way 'at Armazindy jes
Drapped back in her linsey dress,
And grabbed holt her loom, and shet
Her jaws square.—And ef she fret

ARMAZINDY

Any 'bout it—never 'peared
Sign 'at *neighbers* seed er heerd;—
Most folks liked her all the more—
I know *I* did—certain-shore!—
('Course *I'd* knowed her *Pap*, and what
Stock she come of.—Yes, and thought,
And think *yit*, no man on earth
'S worth as much as that girl's worth!)

As fer Jule and Sol, they had
Their sheer!—less o' good than bad!—
Her folks let her go.—They said,
"Spite o' them she'd made her bed
And must sleep in it!"—But she,
'Peared-like, didn't sleep so free
As she ust to—ner so *late*,
Ner so *fine*, I'm here to state!—
Sol wuz pore, of course, and she
Wuzn't ust to poverty—
Ner she didn't 'pear to jes
'Filiate with lonesomeness,—
'Cause Sol *he* wuz off and out
With his th'asher nigh about
Half the time; er, season done,
He'd be off mi-anderun

ARMAZINDY

Round the country, here and there,
Swoppin' hosses.   Well, that-air
Kind o' livin' didn't suit
Jule a bit!—and then, to boot,
She had now the keer o' two
Her own childern—and to do
Her own work and cookin'—yes,
And sometimes fer *hands*, I guess,
Well as fambily of her own.—
Cut her pride clean to the bone!
So how *could* the whole thing end?—
She set down, one night, and penned
A short note, like—'at she sewed
On the childern's blanket—blowed
Out the candle—pulled the door
To close after her—and, shore-
Footed as a cat is, clumb
In a rigg there and left home,
With a man a-drivin' who
"Loved her ever fond and true,"
As her note went on to say,
When Sol read the thing next day.

Raally didn't 'pear to be
Extry waste o' sympathy

ARMAZINDY

Over Sol—pore feller!—Yit,
Sake o' them-air little bit
O' two *orphants*—as you might
Call 'em *then*, by law and right,—
Sol's old friends wuz sorry, and
Tried to hold him out their hand
Same as allus: But he'd flinch—
Tel, jes 'peared-like, inch by inch,
He let *all* holts go; and so
Took to drinkin', don't you know,—
Tel, to make a long tale short,
He wuz fuller than he ort
To 'a' be'n, at work one day
'Bout his th'asher, and give way,
Kindo'-like, and fell and ketched
In the beltin'.

          . . . Rid and fetched
Armazindy to him.—He
Begged me to.—But time 'at she
Reached his side, he smiled and *tried*
To speak.—Couldn't. So he died. . . .
Hands all turned and left her there
And went somers else—*some*where.
Last, she called us back—in clear
Voice as man'll ever hear—

13

ARMAZINDY

Clear and stiddy, 'peared to me,
As her old Pap's ust to be.—
Give us orders what to do
'Bout the body—he'pped us, too.
So it wuz, Sol Stephens passed
In Armazindy's hands at last.
More'n that, she claimed 'at she
Had consent from him to be
Mother to his childern—now
'Thout no parents anyhow.

Yes-sir! and she's *got* 'em, too,—
Folks saw nothin' else 'ud do—
So they let her have *her way*—
Like she's doin' yit to-day!
Years now, I've be'n coaxin' her—
Armazindy Ballenger—
To in-large her fambily
Jes *one* more by takin' *me*—
Which I'm feared she never will,
Though I'm 'lectioneerin' still.

THE OLD TRUNDLE-BED

O THE old trundle-bed where I slept when a boy!
What canopied king might not covet the joy?
The glory and peace of that slumber of mine,
Like a long, gracious rest in the bosom divine:
The quaint, homely couch, hidden close from the light,
But daintily drawn from its hiding at night.
O a nest of delight, from the foot to the head,
Was the queer little, dear little, old trundle-bed!

O the old trundle-bed, where I wondering saw
The stars through the window, and listened with awe
To the sigh of the winds as they tremblingly crept
Through the trees where the robin so restlessly slept:
Where I heard the low, murmurous chirp of the wren,
And the katydid listlessly chirrup again,
Till my fancies grew faint and were drowsily led
Through the maze of the dreams of the old trundle-bed.

THE OLD TRUNDLE-BED

O the old trundle-bed! O the old trundle-bed!
With its plump little pillow, and old-fashioned spread;
Its snowy-white sheets, and the blankets above,
Smoothed down and tucked round with the touches of
    love;
The voice of my mother to lull me to sleep
With the old fairy stories my memories keep
Still fresh as the lilies that bloom o'er the head
Once bowed o'er my own in the old trundle-bed.

NATURAL PERVERSITIES

I am not prone to moralize
   In scientific doubt
On certain facts that Nature tries
   To puzzle us about,—
For I am no philosopher
   Of wise elucidation,
But speak of things as they occur,
   From simple observation.

I notice *little* things—to wit:—
   I never missed a train
Because I didn't *run* for it;
   I never knew it rain
That my umbrella wasn't lent,—
   Or, when in my possession,
The sun but wore, to all intent,
   A jocular expression.

NATURAL PERVERSITIES

I never knew a creditor
   To dun me for a debt
But I was "cramped" or "bu'sted"; or
   I never knew one yet,
When I had plenty in my purse,
   To make the least invasion,—
As I, accordingly perverse,
   Have courted no occasion.

Nor do I claim to comprehend
   What Nature has in view
In giving us the very friend
   To trust we oughtn't to.—
But so it is: The trusty gun
   Disastrously exploded
Is always sure to be the one
   We didn't think was loaded.

Our moaning is another's mirth,—
   And what is worse by half,
We say the funniest thing on earth
   And never raise a laugh:
'Mid friends that love us overwell,
   And sparkling jests and liquor,
Our hearts somehow are liable
   To melt in tears the quicker.

NATURAL PERVERSITIES

We reach the wrong when most we seek
    The right; in like effect,
We stay the strong and not the weak—
    Do most when we neglect.—
Neglected genius—truth be said—
    As wild and quick as tinder,
The more you seek to help ahead
    The more you seem to hinder.

I've known the least the greatest, too—
    And, on the selfsame plan,
The biggest fool I ever knew
    Was quite a little man:
We find we ought, and then we won't—
    We prove a thing, then doubt it,—
Know *everything* but when we don't
    Know *anything* about it.

THE OLD SCHOOL-CHUM

He puts the poem by, to say
His eyes are not themselves to-day!

A sudden glamour o'er his sight—
A something vague, indefinite—

An oft-recurring blur that blinds
The printed meaning of the lines,

And leaves the mind all dusk and dim
In swimming darkness—strange to him!

It is not childishness, I guess,—
Yet something of the tenderness

That used to wet his lashes when
A boy seems troubling him again;—

THE OLD SCHOOL-CHUM

The old emotion, sweet and wild,
That drove him truant when a child,

That he might hide the tears that fell
Above the lesson—"Little Nell."

And so it is he puts aside
The poem he has vainly tried

To follow; and, as one who sighs
In failure, through a poor disguise

Of smiles, he dries his tears, to say
His eyes are not themselves to-day.

WRITIN' BACK TO THE HOME-FOLKS

My dear old friends—It jes beats all,
    The way you write a letter
So's ever' *last* line beats the *first*,
    And ever' *next*-un's better!—
W'y, ever' fool-thing you putt down
    You make so int*e*r*e*st*i*n',
A feller, readin' of 'em all,
    Can't tell which is the *best*-un.

It's all so comfortin' and good,
    'Pears-like I almost *hear* ye
And git more sociabler, you know,
    And hitch my cheer up near ye
And jes smile on ye like the sun
    Acrosst the whole per-rairies
In Aprile when the thaw's begun
    And country couples marries.

WRITIN' BACK TO THE HOME-FOLKS

It's all so good-old-fashioned like
   To *talk* jes like we're *thinkin'*,
Without no hidin' back o' fans
   And giggle-un and winkin',
Ner sizin' how each other's dressed—
   Like some is allus doin',—
"*Is* Marthy Ellen's basque be'n *turned*
   Er shore-enough a new-un!"—

Er "ef Steve's city-friend hain't jes
   'A *lee*tle kindo'-sorto'"—
Er "wears them-air blame' eye-glasses
   Jes 'cause he hadn't ort to?"—
And so straight on, *dad-libitum*,
   Tel all of us feels, *some*way,
Jes like our "comp'ny" wuz the best
   When we git up to come 'way!

That's why I like *old* friends like *you*,—
   Jes 'cause you're so *abidin'*.—
Ef I wuz built to live "*fer keeps*,"
   My principul residin'
Would be amongst the folks 'at kep'
   Me allus *thinkin'* of 'em,
And sorto' eechin' all the time
   To tell 'em how I love 'em.—

WRITIN' BACK TO THE HOME-FOLKS

Sich folks, you know, I jes love so
I wouldn't live without 'em,
Er couldn't even drap asleep
But what I *dreamp'* about 'em,—
And ef we minded God, I guess
We'd *all* love one another
Jes like one famb'ly,—me and Pap
And Madaline and Mother.

THE BLIND GIRL

If I might see his face to-day!—
  He is so happy now!—To hear
His laugh is like a roundelay—
  So ringing-sweet and clear!
His step—I heard it long before
He bounded through the open door
To tell his marriage.—Ah! so kind—
So good he is!—And I—so blind!

But thus he always came to me—
  Me, first of all, he used to bring
His sorrow to—his ecstasy—
  His hopes and everything;
And if I joyed with him or wept,
It was not long *the music* slept,—
And if he sung, or if I played—
Or both,—we were the braver made.

THE BLIND GIRL

I grew to know and understand
    His every word at every call,—
The gate-latch hinted, and his hand
    In mine confessed it all:
He need not speak one word to me—
He need not sigh—I need not see,—
But just the one touch of his palm,
And I would answer—song or psalm.

He wanted recognition—name—
    He hungered so for higher things,—
The altitudes of power and fame,
    And all that fortune brings:
Till, with his great heart fevered thus,
And aching as impetuous,
I almost wished sometimes that *he*
Were blind and patient made, like me.

But he has won!—I knew he would.—
    Once in the mighty Eastern mart,
I knew his music only could
    Be sung in every heart!
And when he proudly sent me this
From out the great metropolis,
I bent above the graven score
And, weeping, kissed it o'er and o'er.—

THE BLIND GIRL

And yet not blither sing the birds
   Than this glad melody,—the tune
As sweetly wedded with the words
   As flowers with middle-June;
Had he not *told* me, I had known
It was composed of love alone—
His love for *her*.—And she can see
His happy face eternally!—

While *I*—O God, forgive, I pray!—
   Forgive me that I did so long
To look upon his face to-day!—
   I know the wish was wrong.—
Yea, I am thankful that my sight
Is shielded safe from such delight:—
I can pray better, with this blur
Of blindness—both for him and her.

WE DEFER THINGS

We say and we say and we say,
    We promise, engage and declare,
Till a year from to-morrow is yesterday,
    And yesterday is—Where?

THE MUSKINGUM VALLEY

The Muskingum Valley!—How longin' the gaze
A feller throws back on its long summer days,
When the smiles of its blossoms and *my* smiles wuz one-
And-the-same, from the rise to the set o' the sun:
Wher' the hills sloped as soft as the dawn down to noon,
And the river run by like an old fiddle-tune,
And the hours glided past as the bubbles 'ud glide,
All so loaferin'-like, 'long the path o' the tide.

In the Muskingum Valley—it 'peared-like the skies
Looked lovin' on me as my own mother's eyes,
While the laughin'-sad song of the stream seemed to be
Like a lullaby angels was wastin' on me—
Tel, swimmin' the air, like the gossamer's thread,
'Twixt the blue underneath and the blue overhead,
My thoughts went astray in that so-to-speak realm
Wher' Sleep bared her breast as a piller fer them.

THE MUSKINGUM VALLEY

In the Muskingum Valley, though far, far away,
I know that the winter is bleak there to-day—
No bloom ner perfume on the brambles er trees—
Wher' the buds ust to bloom, now the icicles freeze.—
That the grass is all hid 'long the side of the road
Wher' the deep snow has drifted and shifted and blowed—
And I feel in my life the same changes is there,—
The frost in my heart, and the snow in my hair.

But, Muskingum Valley! my memory sees
Not the white on the ground, but the green in the trees—
Not the froze'-over gorge, but the current, as clear
And warm as the drop that has jes trickled here;
Not the choked-up ravine, and the hills topped with snow,
But the grass and the blossoms I knowed long ago
When my little bare feet wundered down wher' the stream
In the Muskingum Valley flowed on like a dream.

FOR THIS CHRISTMAS

YE old-time stave that pealeth out
    To Christmas revellers all,
At tavern-tap and wassail-bout,
    And in ye banquet-hall.—
Whiles ye old burden rings again,
    Add yet ye verse, as due:
" God bless you, merry gentlemen "—
    And gentlewomen, too!

A POOR MAN'S WEALTH

A poor man? Yes, I must confess—
No wealth of gold do I possess;
No pastures fine, with grazing kine,
Nor fields of waving grain are mine;
No foot of fat or fallow land
Where rightfully my feet may stand
The while I claim it as my own—
By deed and title, mine alone.

Ah, poor indeed! perhaps you say—
But spare me your compassion, pray!—
When I ride not—with you—I walk
In Nature's company, and talk
With one who will not slight or slur
The child forever dear to her—
And one who answers back, be sure,
With smile for smile, though I am poor.

A POOR MAN'S WEALTH

And while communing thus, I count
An inner wealth of large amount,—
The wealth of honest purpose blent
With Penury's environment,—
The wealth of owing naught to-day
But debts that I would gladly pay,
With wealth of thanks still unexpressed
With cumulative interest.—

A wealth of patience and content—
For all my ways improvident;
A faith still fondly exercised—
For all my plans unrealized;
A wealth of promises that still,
Howe'er I fail, I hope to fill;
A wealth of charity for those
Who pity me my ragged clothes.

A poor man? Yes, I must confess—
No wealth of gold do I possess;
No pastures fine, with grazing kine,
Nor fields of waving grain are mine;
But ah, my friend! I've wealth, no end!
For millionaires might condescend
To bend the knee and envy me
This opulence of poverty.

THE LITTLE RED RIBBON

The little red ribbon, the ring and the rose!
The summer-time comes, and the summer-time goes—
And never a blossom in all of the land
As white as the gleam of her beckoning hand!

The long winter months, and the glare of the snows;
The little red ribbon, the ring and the rose!
And never a glimmer of sun in the skies
As bright as the light of her glorious eyes!

Dreams only are true; but they fade and are gone—
For her face is not here when I waken at dawn;
The little red ribbon, the ring and the rose
Mine only; *hers* only the dream and repose.

I am weary of waiting, and weary of tears,
And my heart wearies, too, all these desolate years,
Moaning over the one only song that it knows,—
The little red ribbon, the ring and the rose!

"HOW DID YOU REST, LAST NIGHT?"

"How did you rest, last night?"—
  I've heard my gran'pap say
Them words a thousand times—that's right—
  Jes them words thataway!
As punctchul-like as morning dast
  To ever heave in sight
Gran'pap 'ud allus haf to ast—
  "How did you rest, last night?"

Us young-uns used to grin,
  At breakfast, on the sly,
And mock the wobble of his chin
  And eyebrows helt so high
And kind: "*How did you rest, last night?*"
  We'd mumble and let on
Our voices trimbled, and our sight
  Wuz dim, and hearin' gone.

"HOW DID YOU REST, LAST NIGHT?"

. . . . . .

Bad as I ust to be,
   All I'm a-wantin' is
As puore and ca'm a sleep fer me
   And sweet a sleep as his!
And so I pray, on Jedgment Day
   To wake, and with its light
See *his* face dawn, and hear him say—
   "How did you rest, last night?"

A GOOD-BYE

"Good-bye, my friend!"
  He takes her hand—
The pressures blend:
    They understand
        But vaguely why, with drooping eye,
        Each moans—"Good-bye!—Good-bye!"

"Dear friend, good-bye!"
  O she could smile
If she might cry
  A little while!—
        She says, "I *ought* to smile—but I—
        Forgive me—*There!*—Good-bye!"

"'Good-bye?' Ah, no:
  I hate," says he,
"These 'good-byes' so!"
  "And *I*," says she,
        "Detest them so—why, I should *die*
        Were this a *real* 'good-bye!'"

WHEN MAIMIE MARRIED

WHEN Maimie married Charley Brown,
Joy took possession of the town;
The young folks swarmed in happy throngs—
They rang the bells—they carolled songs—
They carpeted the steps that led
Into the church where they were wed;
And up and down the altar-stair
They scattered roses everywhere;
When, in her orange-blossom crown,
Queen Maimie married Charley Brown.

So beautiful she was, it seemed
Men, looking on her, dreamed they dreamed;
And he, the holy man who took
Her hand in his, so thrilled and shook,
The gargoyles round the ceiling's rim
Looked down and leered and grinned at him,

WHEN MAIMIE MARRIED

Until he half forgot his part
Of sanctity, and felt his heart
Beat worldward through his sacred gown—
When Maimie married Charley Brown.

The bridesmaids kissed her, left and right—
Fond mothers hugged her with delight—
Young men of twenty-seven were seen
To blush like lads of seventeen,
The while they held her hand to quote
Such sentiments as poets wrote.—
Yea, all the heads that Homage bends
Were bowed to her.—But O my friends,
My hopes went up—*my* heart went down—
When Maimie married—*Charley Brown!*

"THIS DEAR CHILD-HEARTED WOMAN THAT IS DEAD"

I

THIS woman, with the dear child-heart,
   Ye mourn as dead, is—where and what?
With faith as artless as her Art,
        I question not,—

But dare divine, and feel, and know
   Her blessedness—as hath been writ
In allegory.—Even so
        I fashion it:—

II

A stately figure, rapt and awed
   In her new guise of Angelhood,
Still lingered, wistful—knowing God
        Was very good.—

Her thought's fine whisper filled the pause;
   And, listening, the Master smiled,
And lo! the stately angel was
        —A little child.

TO A POET-CRITIC

Yes,—the bee sings—I confess it—
Sweet as honey—Heaven bless it!—
Yit he'd be a *sweeter* singer
Ef he didn't have no stinger.

AN OLD-TIMER

Here where the wayward stream
Is restful as a dream,
   And where the banks o'erlook
A pool from out whose deeps
My pleased face upward peeps,
         I cast my hook.

Silence and sunshine blent!—
A Sabbath-like content
   Of wood and wave;—a free-
Hand landscape grandly wrought
Of Summer's brightest thought
         And mastery.—

For here form, light and shade,
And color—all are laid
   With skill so rarely fine,

AN OLD-TIMER

The eye may even see
The ripple tremblingly
        Lip at the line.

I mark the dragon-fly
Flit waveringly by
  In ever-veering flight,
Till, in a hush profound,
I see him eddy round
        The "cork," and—'light!

Ho! with the boy's faith then
Brimming my heart again,
  And knowing, soon or late,
The "nibble" yet shall roll
Its thrills along the pole,
        I—breathless—wait.

THE SILENT VICTORS

May 30, 1878

*"Dying for victory, cheer on cheer
Thundered on his eager ear."*
       Charles L. Holstein.

I

Deep, tender, firm and true, the Nation's heart
 Throbs for her gallant heroes passed away,
Who in grim Battle's drama played their part,
 And slumber here to-day.—

Warm hearts that beat their lives out at the shrine
 Of Freedom, while our country held its breath
As brave battalions wheeled themselves in line
 And marched upon their death:

When Freedom's Flag, its natal wounds scarce healed,
 Was torn from peaceful winds and flung again

THE SILENT VICTORS

To shudder in the storm of battle-field—
   The elements of men,—

When every star that glittered was a mark
   For Treason's ball, and every rippling bar
Of red and white was sullied with the dark
   And purple stain of war:

When angry guns, like famished beasts of prey,
   Were howling o'er their gory feast of lives,
And sending dismal echoes far away
   To mothers, maids, and wives:—

The mother, kneeling in the empty night,
   With pleading hands uplifted for the son
Who, even as she prayed, had fought the fight—
   The victory had won:

The wife, with trembling hand that wrote to say
   The babe was waiting for the sire's caress—
The letter meeting that upon the way,—
   The babe was fatherless:

The maiden, with her lips, in fancy, pressed
   Against the brow once dewy with her breath,
Now lying numb, unknown, and uncaressed
   Save by the dews of death.

THE SILENT VICTORS

II

What meed of tribute can the poet pay
   The Soldier, but to trail the ivy-vine
Of idle rhyme above his grave to-day
   In epitaph design?—

Or wreathe with laurel-words the icy brows
   That ache no longer with a dream of fame,
But, pillowed lowly in the narrow house,
   Renown'd beyond the name.

The dewy tear-drops of the night may fall,
   And tender morning with her shining hand
May brush them from the grasses green and tall
   That undulate the land.—

Yet song of Peace nor din of toil and thrift,
   Nor chanted honors, with the flowers we heap,
Can yield us hope the Hero's head to lift
   Out of its dreamless sleep:

The dear old flag, whose faintest flutter flies
   A stirring echo through each patriot breast,
Can never coax to life the folded eyes
   That saw its wrongs redressed—

THE SILENT VICTORS

That watched it waver when the fight was hot,
    And blazed with newer courage to its aid,
Regardless of the shower of shell and shot
    Through which the charge was made;—

And when, at last, they saw it plume its wings,
    Like some proud bird in stormy element,
And soar untrammelled on its wanderings,
    They closed in death, content.

III

O mother, you who miss the smiling face
    Of that dear boy who vanished from your sight,
And left you weeping o'er the vacant place
    He used to fill at night,—

Who left you dazed, bewildered, on a day
    That echoed wild huzzas, and roar of guns
That drowned the farewell words you tried to say
    To incoherent ones;—

Be glad and proud you had the life to give—
    Be comforted through all the years to come,—
Your country has a longer life to live,
    Your son a better home.

THE SILENT VICTORS

O widow, weeping o'er the orphaned child,
  Who only lifts his questioning eyes to send
A keener pang to grief unreconciled,—
  Teach him to comprehend

He had a father brave enough to stand
  Before the fire of Treason's blazing gun,
That, dying, he might will the rich old land
  Of Freedom to his son.

And, maiden, living on through lonely years
  In fealty to love's enduring ties,—
With strong faith gleaming through the tender tears
  That gather in your eyes,

Look up! and own, in gratefulness of prayer,
  Submission to the will of Heaven's High Host:—
I see your Angel-soldier pacing there,
  Expectant at his post.—

I see the rank and file of armies vast,
  That muster under one supreme control;
I hear the trumpet sound the signal-blast—
  The calling of the roll—

The grand divisions falling into line
  And forming, under voice of One alone,

THE SILENT VICTORS

Who gives command, and joins with tongue divine
   The hymn that shakes the Throne.

IV

And thus, in tribute to the forms that rest
   In their last camping-ground, we strew the bloom
And fragrance of the flowers they loved the best,
   In silence o'er the tomb.

With reverent hands we twine the Hero's wreath
   And clasp it tenderly on stake or stone
That stands the sentinel for each beneath
   Whose glory is our own.

While in the violet that greets the sun,
   We see the azure eye of some lost boy;
And in the rose the ruddy cheek of one
   We kissed in childish joy,—

Recalling, haply, when he marched away,
   He laughed his loudest though his eyes were wet.—
The kiss he gave his mother's brow that day
   Is there and burning yet:

And through the storm of grief around her tossed,
   One ray of saddest comfort she may see,—

THE SILENT VICTORS

Four hundred thousand sons like hers were lost
   To weeping Liberty.

  .   .   .   .

But draw aside the drapery of gloom,
   And let the sunshine chase the clouds away
And gild with brighter glory every tomb
   We decorate to-day:

And in the holy silence reigning round,
   While prayers of perfume bless the atmosphere,
Where loyal souls of love and faith are found,
   Thank God that Peace is here!

And let each angry impulse that may start,
   Be smothered out of every loyal breast;
And, rocked within the cradle of the heart,
   Let every sorrow rest.

UP AND DOWN OLD BRANDYWINE

Up and down old Brandywine,
　In the days 'at's past and gone—
With a dad-burn hook-and-line
　And a saplin'-pole—i swawn!
　　I've had more fun, to the square
　　Inch, than ever *any*where!
　　Heaven to come can't discount *mine*,
　　Up and down old Brandywine!

Hain't no sense in *wishin'*—yit
　Wisht to goodness I *could* jes
"Gee" the blame' world round and **git**
　Back to that old happiness!—
　　Kindo' drive back in the shade
　　"The old Covered Bridge" there **laid**
　　'Crosst the crick, and sorto' **soak**
　　My soul over, hub and spoke!

UP AND DOWN OLD BRANDYWINE

Honest, now!—it hain't no *dream*
  'At I'm wantin',—but *the fac's*
As they wuz; the same old stream,
  And the same old times, i jacks!—
    Gimme back my bare feet—and
    Stonebruise too!—And scratched and
      tanned!—
    And let hottest dog-days shine
    Up and down old Brandywine!

In and on betwixt the trees
  'Long the banks, pour down yer noon,
Kindo' curdled with the breeze
  And the yallerhammer's tune;
    And the smokin', chokin' dust
    O' the turnpike at its wusst—
    Saturd'ys, say, when it seems
    Road's jes jammed with country teams!

Whilse the old town, fur away
  'Crosst the hazy pastur'-land,
Dozed-like in the heat o' day
  Peaceful' as a hired hand.
    Jolt the gravel th'ough the floor
    O' the ole bridge!—grind and roar

UP AND DOWN OLD BRANDYWINE

    With yer blame' percession-line—
    Up and down old Brandywine!

Souse me and my new straw hat
    Off the foot-log!—what *I* care?—
Fist shoved in the crown o' that—
    Like the old Clown ust to wear.—
        Wouldn't swop it fer a' old
        Gin-u-wine raal crown o' gold?—
        Keep yer *King* ef you'll gim me
        Jes the boy I ust to be!

Spill my fishin'-worms! er steal
    My best "goggle-eye!"—but you
Can't lay hands on joys I feel
    Nibblin' like they ust to do!
        So, in memory, to-day
        Same old ripple lips away
        At my "cork" and saggin' line,
        Up and down old Brandywine!

There the logs is, round the hill,
    Where "Old Irvin" ust to lift
Out sunfish from daylight till
    Dewfall—'fore he'd leave "The Drift"

And give *us* a chance—and then
Kindo' fish back home again,
Ketchin' 'em jes left and right
Where *we* hadn't got "a bite"!

Er, 'way windin' out and in,—
  Old path th'ough the iurnweeds
And dog-fennel to yer chin—
  Then come suddent, th'ough the reeds
    And cattails, smack into where
    Them-air woods-hogs ust to scare
    Us clean 'crosst the County-line,
    Up and down old Brandywine!

But the dim roar o' the dam
  It 'ud coax us furder still
To'rds the old race, slow and ca'm,
  Slidin' on to Huston's mill—
    Where, I 'spect, "the Freeport crowd"
    Never *warmed* to us er 'lowed
    We wuz quite so overly
    Welcome as we aimed to be.

Still it 'peared-like ever'thing—
  Fur away from home as *there*—

UP AND DOWN OLD BRANDYWINE

Had more *relish*-like, i jing!—
  Fish in stream, er bird in air!
    O them rich old bottom-lands,
      Past where Cowden's School-house stands!
      Wortermelons—*master-mine!*
      Up and down old Brandywine!

And sich pop-paws!—Lumps o' raw
  Gold and green,—jes oozy th'ough
With ripe yaller—like you've saw
  Custard-pie with no crust to:
    And jes *gorges* o' wild plums,
    Till a feller'd suck his thumbs
    Clean up to his elbows! *My!—*
    Me some more er lem me die!

Up and down old Brandywine! . . .
  Stripe me with pokeberry-juice!—
Flick me with a pizen-vine
  And yell "*Yip!*" and lem me loose!
    —Old now as I then wuz young,
    'F I could sing as I *have* sung,
    Song 'ud shorely ring *dee-vine*
    Up and down old Brandywine!

THREE SINGING FRIENDS

I

LEE O. HARRIS

SCHOOLMASTER and Songmaster! Memory
   Enshrines thee with an equal love, for thy
   Duality of gifts,—thy pure and high
Endowments—Learning rare, and Poesy.
These were as mutual handmaids, serving thee,
   Throughout all seasons of the years gone by,
   With all enduring joys 'twixt earth and sky—
In turn shared nobly with thy friends and me.
Thus is it that thy clear song, ringing on,
   Is endless inspiration, fresh and free
      As the old Mays at verge of June sunshine;
And musical as then, at dewy dawn,
   The robin hailed us, and all twinklingly
      Our one path wandered under wood and vine.

THREE SINGING FRIENDS

II

BENJ. S. PARKER

Thy rapt song makes of Earth a realm of light
   And shadow mystical as some dreamland
     Arched with unfathomed azure—vast and grand
With splendor of the morn; or dazzling bright
With orient noon; or strewn with stars of night
   Thick as the daisies blown in grasses fanned
     By odorous midsummer breezes and
Showered over by all bird-songs exquisite.
This is thy voice's beatific art—
   To make melodious all things below,
     Calling through them, from far, diviner space,
Thy clearer hail to us.—The faltering heart
   Thou cheerest; and thy fellow-mortal so
     Fares onward under Heaven with lifted face.

III

JAMES NEWTON MATTHEWS

Bard of our Western world!—its prairies wide,
   With edging woods, lost creeks and hidden ways;
   Its isolated farms, with roundelays

Of orchard warblers heard on every side;
Its cross-road school-house, wherein still abide
    Thy fondest memories,—since there thy gaze
      First fell on classic verse; and thou, in praise
Of that, didst find thine own song glorified.
So singing, smite the strings and counterchange
    The lucently melodious drippings of
      Thy happy harp, from airs of "Tempe Vale,"
To chirp and trill of lowliest flight and range,
    In praise of our To-day and home and love—
      Thou meadow-lark no less than nightingale.

A NOON LULL

'Possum in de 'tater-patch;
  Chicken-hawk a-hangin'
Stiddy 'bove de stable-lot,
  An' cyarpet-loom a-bangin'!
Hi! Mr. Hoppergrass, chawin' yo' terbacker,
Flick ye wid er buggy-whirp yer spit er little blacker!

Niggah in de roas'in'-yeers,
  Whiskers in de shuckin';
Weasel croppin' mighty shy,
  But ole hen a-cluckin'!
—What's got de matter er de mule-colt now?
Drapt in de turnip-hole, chasin' f'um de cow!

A WINDY DAY

The dawn was a dawn of splendor,
   And the blue of the morning skies
Was as placid and deep and tender
   As the blue of a baby's eyes;
The sunshine flooded the mountain,
   And flashed over land and sea
Like the spray of a glittering fountain.—
   But the wind—the wind—Ah me!

Like a weird invisible spirit,
   It swooped in its airy flight;
And the earth, as the stress drew near it,
   Quailed as in mute affright;
The grass in the green fields quivered—
   The waves of the smitten brook
Chillily shuddered and shivered,
   And the reeds bowed down and shook.

A WINDY DAY

Like a sorrowful miserere
It sobbed, and it blew and blew,
Till the leaves on the trees looked weary,
And my prayers were weary, too;
And then, like the sunshine's glimmer
That failed in the awful strain,
All the hope of my eyes grew dimmer
In a spatter of spiteful rain.

MY HENRY

He's jes a great, big, awk'ard, hulkin'
Feller,—humped, and sorto' sulkin'-
Like, and ruther still-appearin'—
Kind-as-ef he wuzn't keerin'
    Whether school helt out er not—
    That's my Henry, to a dot!

Allus kindo' liked him—whether
Childern, er growed-up together!
Fifteen year' ago and better,
'Fore he ever knowed a letter,
    Run acrosst the little fool
    In my Primer-class at school.

When the Teacher wuzn't lookin',
He'd be th'owin' wads; er crookin'
Pins; er sprinklin' pepper, more'n
Likely, on the stove; er borin'
    Gimlet-holes up thue his desk—
    Nothin' *that* boy wouldn't resk!

MY HENRY

But, somehow, as I was goin'
On to say, he seemed so knowin',
Other ways, and cute and cunnin'—
Allus wuz a notion runnin'
>Thue my giddy, fool-head he
>Jes had be'n cut out fer me!

Don't go much on *prophesyin'*,
But last night whilse I wuz fryin'
Supper, with that man a-pitchin'
Little Marthy round the kitchen,
>Think-says-I, "Them baby's eyes
>Is my Henry's, jes p'cise!"

THE SONG I NEVER SING

As when in dreams we sometimes hear
   A melody so faint and fine
And musically sweet and clear,
It flavors all the atmosphere
   With harmony divine,—
      So, often in my waking dreams,
      I hear a melody that seems
      Like fairy voices whispering
      To me the song I never sing.

Sometimes when brooding o'er the years
   My lavish youth has thrown away—
When all the glowing past appears
But as a mirage that my tears
   Have crumbled to decay,—
      I thrill to find the ache and pain
      Of my remorse is stilled again,
      As, forward bent and listening,
      I hear the song I never sing.

THE SONG I NEVER SING

A murmuring of rhythmic words,
  Adrift on tunes whose currents flow
Melodious with the trill of birds,
And far-off lowing of the herds
    In lands of long ago;
      And every sound the truant loves
      Comes to me like the coo of doves
      When first in blooming fields of Spring
      I heard the song I never sing.

The echoes of old voices, wound
  In limpid streams of laughter where
The river Time runs bubble-crowned,
And giddy eddies ripple round
    The lilies growing there;
      Where roses, bending o'er the brink,
      Drain their own kisses as they drink,
      And ivies climb and twine and cling
      About the song I never sing.

An ocean-surge of sound that falls
  As though a tide of heavenly art
Had tempested the gleaming halls
And crested o'er the golden walls
    In showers on my heart. . . .

THE SONG I NEVER SING

    Thus—thus, with open arms and eyes
    Uplifted toward the alien skies,
    Forgetting every earthly thing,
    I hear the song I never sing.

O nameless lay, sing clear and strong,
  Pour down thy melody divine
Till purifying floods of song
Have washed away the stains of wrong
  That dim this soul of mine!
    O woo me near and nearer thee,
    Till my glad lips may catch the key,
    And, with a voice unwavering,
    Join in the song I never sing.

TO EDGAR WILSON NYE

O "WILLIAM,"—in thy blithe companionship
   What liberty is mine—what sweet release
   From clamorous strife, and yet what boisterous peace!
Ho! ho! it is thy fancy's finger-tip
That dints the dimple now, and kinks the lip
   That scarce may sing, in all this glad increase
   Of merriment! So, pray-thee, do not cease
To cheer me thus;—for, underneath the quip
Of thy droll sorcery, the wrangling fret
   Of all distress is stilled—no syllable
Of sorrow vexeth me—no tear-drops wet
   My teeming lids save those that leap to tell
Thee thou'st a guest that overweepeth, yet
   Only because thou jokest overwell.

LITTLE DAVID

The mother of the little boy that sleeps
Has blest assurance, even as she weeps:
She knows her little boy has now no pain—
No further ache, in body, heart or brain;
All sorrow is lulled for him—all distress
Passed into utter peace and restfulness.—
All health that heretofore has been denied—
All happiness, all hope, and all beside
Of childish longing, now he clasps and keeps
In voiceless joy—the little boy that sleeps.

OUT OF THE HITHERWHERE

Out of the hitherwhere into the YON—
The land that the Lord's love rests upon;
Where one may rely on the friends he meets,
And the smiles that greet him along the streets:
Where the mother that left you years ago
Will lift the hands that were folded so,
And put them about you, with all the love
And tenderness you are dreaming of.

Out of the hitherwhere into the YON—
Where all of the friends of your youth have gone,—
Where the old schoolmate that laughed with you,
Will laugh again as he used to do,
Running to meet you, with such a face
As lights like a moon the wondrous place
Where God is living, and glad to live,
Since He is the Master and may forgive.

OUT OF THE HITHERWHERE

Out of the hitherwhere into the YON!—
Stay the hopes we are leaning on—
You, Divine, with Your merciful eyes
Looking down from the far-away skies,—
Smile upon us, and reach and take
Our worn souls Home for the old home's sake.—
And so Amen,—for our all seems gone
Out of the hitherwhere into the YON.

RABBIT IN THE CROSS-TIES

Rabbit in the cross-ties.—
 Punch him out—quick!
Git a twister on him
 With a long prong stick.
Watch him on the south side—
 Watch him on the—Hi!—
There he goes! Sic him, Tige!
 Yi! Yi!! Yi!!!

SERENADE—TO NORA

THE moonlight is failin'—
The sad stars are palin'—
The black wings av night are a-dhroopin' an' trailin';
　　The wind's miserere
　　Sounds lonesome an' dreary;
The katydid's dumb an' the nightingale's weary.

　　Troth, Nora! I'm wadin'
　　The grass an' paradin'
The dews at your dure, wid my swate serenadin',
　　Alone and forsaken,
　　Whilst you're never wakin'
To tell me you're wid me an' I am mistaken!

　　Don't think that my singin'
　　It's wrong to be flingin'
Forninst av the dreams that the Angels are bringin';
　　For if your pure spirit
　　Might waken and hear it,
You'd never be draamin' the Saints could come near it!

SERENADE—TO NORA

Then lave off your slaapin'—
The pulse av me's laapin'
To have the two eyes av yez down on me paapin'.
Och, Nora! It's hopin'
Your windy ye'll open
And light up the night where the heart av me's gropin'.

THE LITTLE WHITE HEARSE

As the little white hearse went glimmering by—
  The man on the coal-cart jerked his lines,
And smutted the lid of either eye,
  And turned and stared at the business signs;
    And the street-car driver stopped and beat
    His hands on his shoulders, and gazed up-street
    Till his eye on the long track reached the sky—
    As the little white hearse went glimmering by.

As the little white hearse went glimmering by—
  A stranger petted a ragged child
In the crowded walks, and she knew not why,
  But he gave her a coin for the way she smiled;
    And a boot-black thrilled with a pleasure strange,
    As a customer put back his change
    With a kindly hand and a grateful sigh,
    As the little white hearse went glimmering by.

THE LITTLE WHITE HEARSE

As the little white hearse went glimmering by—
   A man looked out of a window dim,
And his cheeks were wet and his heart was dry,
   For a dead child even were dear to him!
      And he thought of his empty life, and said:—
      "Loveless alive, and loveless dead—
      Nor wife nor child in earth or sky!"
      As the little white hearse went glimmering by.

WHAT REDRESS

I PRAY you, do not use this thing
For vengeance; but if questioning
What wound, when dealt your humankind,
Goes deepest,—surely he will find
Who wrongs *you*, loving *him* no less—
There's nothing hurts like tenderness.

DREAMER, SAY

DREAMER, say, will you dream for me
   A wild sweet dream of a foreign land,
Whose border sips of a foaming sea
   With lips of coral and silver sand;
Where warm winds loll on the shady deeps,
   Or lave themselves in the tearful mist
The great wild wave of the breaker weeps
   O'er crags of opal and amethyst?

Dreamer, say, will you dream a dream
   Of tropic shades in the lands of shine,
Where the lily leans o'er an amber stream
   That flows like a rill of wasted wine,—
Where the palm-trees, lifting their shields of green,
   Parry the shafts of the Indian sun
Whose splintering vengeance falls between
   The reeds below where the waters run?

DREAMER, SAY

Dreamer, say, will you dream of love
   That lives in a land of sweet perfume,
Where the stars drip down from the skies above
   In molten spatters of bud and bloom?
Where never the weary eyes are wet,
   And never a sob in the balmy air,
And only the laugh of the paroquet
   Breaks the sleep of the silence there?

WHEN LIDE MARRIED *HIM*

When Lide married *him*—w'y, she had to jes dee-fy
The whole popilation!—But she never bat' an eye!
Her parents begged, and *threatened*—she must give him
　　up—that *he*
Wuz jes "a common drunkard!"—And he *wuz*,
　　appearantly.—
　　　　　Swore they'd chase him off the place
　　　　　Ef he ever showed his face—
Long after she'd *eloped* with him and *married* him fer
　　shore!—
When Lide married *him*, it wuz "*Katy, bar the door!*"

When Lide married *him*—Well! she had to go and be
A *hired girl* in town somewheres—while he tromped
　　round to see
What *he* could git that *he* could do,—you might say, jes
　　sawed wood
From door to door!—that's what he done—'cause that
　　wuz best he could!

WHEN LIDE MARRIED *HIM*

And the strangest thing, i jing!
Wuz, he didn't *drink* a thing,—
But jes got down to bizness, like he someway *wanted* to,
When Lide married *him*, like they warned her *not* to do!

When Lide married *him*—er, ruther, *had* be'n married
A little up'ards of a year—some feller come and carried
That *hired girl* away with him—a ruther *stylish* feller
In a bran-new green spring-wagon, with the wheels striped red and yeller:
And he whispered, as they driv
To'rds the country, "*Now we'll live!*"—
And *somepin' else* she *laughed* to hear, though both her eyes wuz dim,
'Bout "*trustin' Love and Heav'n above*, sence Lide married *him!*"

MY BRIDE THAT IS TO BE

O Soul of mine, look out and see
My bride, my bride that is to be!—
  Reach out with mad, impatient hands,
And draw aside futurity
As one might draw a veil aside—
  And so unveil her where she stands
Madonna-like and glorified—
  The queen of undiscovered lands
Of love, to where she beckons me—
My bride, my bride that is to be.

The shadow of a willow-tree
  That wavers on a garden-wall
  In summer-time may never fall
In attitude as gracefully
As my fair bride that is to be;—
  Nor ever Autumn's leaves of brown
As lightly flutter to the lawn
As fall her fairy-feet upon
  The path of love she loiters down.—

MY BRIDE THAT IS TO BE

O'er drops of dew she walks, and yet
Not one may stain her sandal wet—
Ay, she might *dance* upon the way
Nor crush a single drop to spray,
So airy-like she seems to me,—
My bride, my bride that is to be.

I know not if her eyes are light
As summer skies or dark as night,—
I only know that they are dim
   With mystery: In vain I peer
    To make their hidden meaning clear,
     While o'er their surface, like a tear
That ripples to the silken brim,
A look of longing seems to swim
   All worn and weary-like to me;
And then, as suddenly, my sight
Is blinded with a smile so bright,
   Through folded lids I still may see
   My bride, my bride that is to be.

Her face is like a night of June
Upon whose brow the crescent-moon
Hangs pendent in a diadem
Of stars, with envy lighting them.—
   And, like a wild cascade, her hair

MY BRIDE THAT IS TO BE

Floods neck and shoulder, arm and wrist,
Till only through a gleaming mist
   I seem to see a Siren there,
With lips of love and melody
   And open arms and heaving breast
   Wherein I fling myself to rest,
The while my heart cries hopelessly
For my fair bride that is to be.

  .   .   .   .   .   .

Nay, foolish heart and blinded eyes!
My bride hath need of no disguise.—
   But, rather, let her come to me
In such a form as bent above
   My pillow when, in infancy,
I knew not anything but love.—
O let her come from out the lands
   Of Womanhood—not fairy isles,—
And let her come with Woman's hands
   And Woman's eyes of tears and smiles,—
With Woman's hopefulness and grace
Of patience lighting up her face:
And let her diadem be wrought
Of kindly deed and prayerful thought,
That ever over all distress
May beam the light of cheerfulness.—

MY BRIDE THAT IS TO BE

And let her feet be brave to fare
The labyrinths of doubt and care,
That, following, my own may find
The path to Heaven God designed.—
O let her come like this to me—
My bride—my bride that is to be.

"RINGWORM FRANK"

Jest Frank Reed's his *real* name—though
  Boys all calls him "Ringworm Frank,"
'Cause he allus *runs round* so.—
  No man can't tell where to bank
    Frank'll be,
      Next you see
  Er *hear* of him!—Drat his melts!—
  That man's allus *somers else!*

We're old pards.—But Frank he jest
  Can't stay still!—Wuz *prosper'n'* here,
But lit out on furder West
  Somers on a ranch, last year:
     Never heard
     Nary a word
  How he liked it, tel to-day,
  Got this card, reads thisaway:—

"RINGWORM FRANK"

"Dad-burn climate out here makes
　Me homesick all Winter long,
And when Springtime *comes*, it takes
　Two pee-wees to sing one song,—
　　　One sings *'pee,'*
　　　　　And the other one *'wee!'*
Stay right where you air, old pard.—
Wisht *I* wuz this postal card!"

AN EMPTY GLOVE

I

An empty glove—long withering in the grasp
  Of Time's cold palm. I lift it to my lips,—
And lo, once more I thrill beneath its clasp,
  In fancy, as with odorous finger-tips
    It reaches from the years that used to be
    And proffers back love, life and all, to me.

II

Ah! beautiful she was beyond belief:
  Her face was fair and lustrous as the moon's;
Her eyes—too large for small delight or grief,—
  The smiles of them were Laughter's afternoons;
    Their tears were April showers, and their love—
    All sweetest speech swoons ere it speaks thereof.

AN EMPTY GLOVE

III

White-fruited cocoa shown against the shell
    Were not so white as was her brow below
The cloven tresses of the hair that fell
    Across her neck and shoulders of nude snow;
        Her cheeks—chaste pallor, with a crimson stain—
        Her mouth was like a red rose rinsed with rain.

IV

And this was she my fancy held as good—
    As fair and lovable—in every wise
As peerless in pure worth of womanhood
    As was her wondrous beauty in men's eyes.—
        Yet, all alone, I kiss this empty glove—
        The poor husk of the hand I loved—and love.

OUR OWN

They walk here with us, hand-in-hand;
    We gossip, knee-by-knee;
They tell us all that they have planned—
    Of all their joys to be,—
And, laughing, leave us: And, to-day,
    All desolate we cry
Across wide waves of voiceless graves—
    Good-bye! Good-bye! Good-bye!

MAKE-BELIEVE AND CHILD-PLAY

THE FROG

Who am I but the Frog—the Frog!
  My realm is the dark bayou,
And my throne is the muddy and moss-grown log
  That the poison-vine clings to—
And the black-snakes slide in the slimy tide
  Where the ghost of the moon looks blue.

What am I but a King—a King!—
  For the royal robes I wear—
A sceptre, too, and a signet-ring,
  As vassals and serfs declare:
And a voice, god wot, that is equalled not
  In the wide world anywhere!

I can talk to the Night—the Night!—
  Under her big black wing
She tells me the tale of the world outright,
  And the secret of everything;
For she knows you all, from the time you crawl,
  To the doom that death will bring.

THE FROG

The Storm swoops down, and he blows—and blows,—
  While I drum on his swollen cheek,
And croak in his angered eye that glows
  With the lurid lightning's streak;
While the rushes drown in the watery frown
  That his bursting passions leak.

And I can see through the sky—the sky—
  As clear as a piece of glass;
And I can tell you the how and why
  Of the things that come to pass—
And whether the dead are there instead,
  Or under the graveyard grass.

To your Sovereign lord all hail—all hail!—
  To your Prince on his throne so grim!
Let the moon swing low, and the high stars trail
  Their heads in the dust to him;
And the wide world sing: Long live the King,
  And grace to his royal whim!

"TWIGGS AND TUDENS"

If my old school-chum and room-mate John Skinner is alive to-day—and no doubt he *is* alive, and quite so, being, when last heard from, the very alert and effective Train Dispatcher at Butler, Indiana,—he will not have forgotten a certain night in early June (the 8th) of 1870, in "Old Number 'Leven" of the Dunbar House, Greenfield, when he and I sat the long night through, getting ready a famous issue of our old school-paper, "The Criterion." And he will remember, too, the queer old man who occupied, but that one night, the room just opposite our own, Number 13. For reasons wholly aside from any superstitious dread connected with the numerals, 13 was not a desirable room; its locality was alien to all accommodations, and its comforts, like its furnishings, were extremely meagre. In fact, it was the room usually assigned to the tramp-printer, who, in those days, was an institution; or again, it was the local habitation

"TWIGGS AND TUDENS"

of the oft-recurring transient customer who was too incapacitated to select a room himself when he retired—or rather, when he was personally retired by "the hostler," as the gentlemanly night-clerk of that era was habitually designated.

As both Skinner and myself—between fitful terms of school—had respectively served as "printer's devil" in the two rival newspaper offices of the town, it was natural for us to find a ready interest in anything pertaining to the newspaper business; and so it was, perhaps, that we had been selected, by our own approval and that of our fellow-students of The Graded Schools, to fill the rather exalted office of editing "The Criterion." Certain it is that the rather abrupt rise from the lowly duties of the "roller" to the editorial management of a paper of our own (even if issued in handwriting) we accepted as a natural right; and, vested in our new power of office, we were largely "shaping the whisper of the throne" about our way.

And upon this particular evening it was, as John and I had fairly squared ourselves for the work of the night, that we heard the clatter and shuffle of feet on the side-stairs, and, an instant later, the hostler establishing some poor unfortunate in 13, just across the hall.

"Listen!" said John, as we heard an old man's voice

through the open transom of our door,—"listen at that!"

It was an utterance peculiarly refined, in language as well as intonation. A low, mild, rather apologetic voice, gently assuring the hostler that "everything was very snug and comfortable indeed—so far as the *compartment* was concerned—but would not the *attendant* kindly supply a better light, together with pen-and-ink—and just a sheet or two of paper,—if he would be so very good as to find a pardon for so very troublesome a guest."

"Hain't no writin'-paper," said the hostler, briefly,—"and the big lamps is all in use. These fellers here in 'Leven might let you have some paper and—Hain't *you* got a lead-pencil?"

"Oh, no matter!" came the impatient yet kindly answer of the old voice—"no matter at all, my good fellow! —Good night—good night!"

We waited till the sullen, clumpy footsteps down the hall and stair had died away.

Then Skinner, with a handful of foolscap, opened our door; and, with an indorsing smile from me, crossed the hall and tapped at 13—was admitted—entered, and very quietly closed the door behind him, evidently that I might not be disturbed.

"TWIGGS AND TUDENS"

I wrote on in silence for quite a time. It was, in fact, a full half-hour before John had returned,—and with a face and eye absolutely blazing with delight.

"An old printer," whispered John, answering my look,—"and we're in luck:—He's a *genius*, 'y God! and an Englishman, and knows Dickens *personally*—used to write races with him, and's got a manuscript of his in his 'portmanteau,' as he calls an old oil-cloth knapsack with one lung clean gone. Excuse this extra light.—Old man's lamp's like a sore eye, and he's going to touch up the Dickens sketch for *us*! Hear?—*For us*—for 'The Criterion.' Says he can't sleep—he's in distress—has a presentiment—some dear friend is dying—or dead now—and he must write—*write!*"

This is, in briefest outline, the curious history of the subjoined sketch, especially curious for the reason that the following morning's cablegram announced that the great novelist, Charles Dickens, had been stricken suddenly and seriously the night previous. On the day of this announcement—even as "The Criterion" was being read to perfunctorily interested visitors of The Greenfield Graded Schools—came the further announcement of Mr. Dickens's death. The old printer's manuscript, here reproduced, is, as originally, captioned—

"TWIGGS AND TUDENS"

TWIGGS AND TUDENS

"Now who'd want a more cosier little home than me and Tude's got here?" asked Mr. Twiggs, as his twinkling eyes swept caressingly around the cheery little room in which he, alone, stood one chill December evening as the great St. Paul's was drawling six.

"This ain't no princely hall with all its gorgeous paraphanaly, as the play-bills says; but it's what I calls a' 'interior,' which for meller comfort and cheerful surroundin's ain't to be ekalled by no other 'flat' on the boundless, never-endin' stage of this existence!" And as the exuberant Mr. Twiggs rendered this observation, he felt called upon to smile and bow most graciously to an invisible audience, whose wild approval he in turn interpreted by an enthusiastic clapping of his hands and the cry of "Ongcore!" in a dozen different keys—this strange acclamation being made the more grotesque by a great green parrot perched upon the mantel, which, in a voice less musical than penetrating, chimed in with "Hooray for Twiggs and Tudens!" a very great number of times.

"Tude's a queer girl," said Mr. Twiggs, subsiding into a reflective calm, broken only by the puffing of his pipe,

"TWIGGS AND TUDENS"

and the occasional articulation of a thought, as it loitered through his mind. "Tude's a queer girl!—a werry queer girl!" repeated Mr. Twiggs, pausing again, with a long whiff at his pipe, and marking the graceful swoop the smoke made as it dipped and disappeared up the wide, black-throated chimney; and then, as though dropping into confidence with the great fat kettle on the coals, that steamed and bubbled with some inner paroxysm, he added, "And queer and nothink short, is the lines for Tude, eh?

"Now s'posin'," he continued, leaning forward and speaking in a tone whose careful intonation might have suggested a more than ordinary depth of wisdom and sagacity,—" s'posin' a pore chap like me, as ain't no property only this-'ere 'little crooked house,' as Tude calls it, and some o' the properties I 'andles at the Drury—as I was a-sayin',—s'posin' now a' old rough chap like me was jest to tell her all about herself, and who she is and all, and not no kith or kin o' mine, let alone a daughter, as *she* thinks—What do you reckon now 'ud be the upshot, eh?" And as Mr. Twiggs propounded this mysterious query he jabbed the poker prankishly in the short-ribs of the grate, at which the pot, as though humoring a joke it failed to comprehend wholly, set up a chuckling of such asthmatic violence that its smothered cachinna-

"TWIGGS AND TUDENS"

tions tilted its copper lid till Mr. Twiggs was obliged to dash a cup of water in its face.

"And Tude's a-comin' of a' age, too," continued Mr. Twiggs, "when a more tenderer pertecter than a father, so to speak, wouldn't be out o' keepin' with the nat'ral order o' things, seein' as how she's sorto' startin' for herself-like now. And it's a question in my mind, if it ain't my bounden duty as her father—or ruther, who has been a father to her all her life—to kindo' tell her jest how things is, and all—and how *I* am, and everythink,—and how I feel as though I ort'o stand by her, as I allus have, and allus *have* had her welfare in view, and kindo' feel as how I allus—ort'o kindo'—ort'o kindo'"—and here Mr. Twiggs's voice fell into silence so abruptly that the drowsy parrot started from its trance-like quiet and cried "Ortokindo! Ortokindo!" with such a strength of seeming mockery that it was brushed violently to the floor by the angry hand of Mr. Twiggs and went backing awkwardly beneath the table.

"Blow me," said Mr. Twiggs, "if the knowin' impidence of that-'ere bird ain't astonishin'!" And then, after a serious controversy with the draught of his pipe, he went on with his deliberations.

"Lor! it were jest scrumptious to see Tude in 'The Iron Chest' last night! Now, I ain't no actur myself,—

I've been on, of course, a thousand times as 'fillin',' 'sogers' and 'peasants' and the like, where I never had no lines, on'y in the 'choruses'; but if I don't know nothin' but 'All hail!—All hail!' I've had the experience of bein' under the baleful hinfluence of the hoppery-glass, and I'm free to say it air a ticklish position and no mistake. But *Tude!* w'y, bless you, she warn't the first bit flustered, was she? 'Peared-like she jest felt perfectly at home-like—like her mother afore her! And I'm dashed if I didn't feel the cold chills a-creepin' and a-crawlin' when she was a-singin' 'Down by the river there grows a green willer and a-weepin' all night with the bank for her piller'; and when she come to the part about wantin' to be buried there 'while the winds was a-blowin' close by the stream where her tears was a-flowin', and over her corpse to keep the green willers growin',' I'm d—d if I didn't blubber right out!" And as the highly sympathetic Mr. Twiggs delivered this acknowledgment, he stroked the inner corners of his eyes, and rubbed his thumb and finger on his trousers.

"It were a tryin' thing, though," he went on, his mellow features settling into a look not at all in keeping with his shiny complexion—"it were a tryin' thing, and it *air* a tryin' thing to see them lovely arms o' hern a-twinin' so lovin'-like around that-'ere Stanley's neck

"TWIGGS AND TUDENS"

and a-kissin' of him—as she's obleeged to do, of course—as the 'properties' of the play demands; but I'm blowed if she wouldn't do it quite so nat'ral-like I'd feel easier. Blow me!" he broke off savagely, starting up and flinging his pipe in the ashes, "I'm about a-comin' to the conclusion I ain't got no more courage'n a blasted school-boy! Here I am old enough to be her father—mighty nigh it—and yet I'm actually afeard to speak up and tell her jest how things is, and all, and how I feel like I—like I—ort'o—ort'o—"

"*Ortokindo! Ortokindo!*" shrieked the parrot, clinging in a reversed position to the under-round of a chair. —"*Ortokindo! Ortokindo! Tude's come home!—Tude's come home!*" And as though in happy proof of this latter assertion, the gentle Mr. Twiggs found his chubby neck encircled by a pair of rosy arms, and felt upon his cheek the sudden pressure of a pair of lips that thrilled his old heart to the core. And then the noisy bird dropped from its perch and marched pompously from its place of concealment, trailing its rusty wings and shrieking, "Tude's come home!" at the top of its brazen voice.

"Shet up!" screamed Mr. Twiggs, with a pretended gust of rage, kicking lamely at the feathered oracle; "I'll 'Tude's-come-home' ye! W'y, a feller can't hear his *ears* for your infernal squawkin'!" And then, turning toward the serious eyes that peered rebukingly into his own, his voice fell gentle as a woman's: "Well, there, Tudens, I beg parding; I do indeed. Don't look at me thataway. I know I'm a great, rough, good-for—" But a warm, swift kiss cut short the utterance; and as the girl drew back, still holding the bright old face between her tender palms, he said simply, "You're a queer girl, Tudens; a queer girl."

"Ha! am I?" said the girl, in quite evident heroics and quotation, starting back with a theatrical flourish and falling into a fantastic attitude.—"'Troth, I am sorry for it; me poor father's heart is bursting with gratichude, and he would fain ease it by pouring out his thanks to his benefactor.'"

"Werry good! Werry good, indeed!" said Mr. Twiggs, gazing wistfully upon the graceful figure of the girl. "You're a-growin' more wonderful' clever in your 'presence' every day, Tude. You don't think o' nothink else but your actin', do ye, now?" And, as Mr. Twiggs concluded his observations, a something very like a sigh came faltering from his lips.

"Why, listen there! Ah-ha!" laughed Tude, clapping her hands and dancing gayly around his chair.—"Why, you old melancholy Dane, you! are you actually *sighing?*"

"TWIGGS AND TUDENS"

Then, dropping into a tragic air of deep contrition, she continued: "'But, believe me, I would not question you, but to console you, Wilford. I would scorn to pry into any one's grief, much more yours, Wilford, to satisfy a busy curiosity.'"

"Oh, don't, Tude; don't *rehearse* like that at me!—I can't a-bear it." And the serious Mr. Twiggs held out his hand as though warding off a blow. At this appeal the girl's demeanor changed to one of tenderest solicitude.

"Why, Pop'm," she said, laying her hand on his shoulder, "I did not mean to vex you—forgive me. I was only trying to be happy, as I ought, although my own heart is this very minute heavy—very heavy—very. —No, no; I don't mean that—but, Father, Father, I have not been dutiful."

"W'y, yes, you have," broke in Mr. Twiggs, smothering the heavy exclamation in his handkerchief. "You ain't been ondutiful, nor nothink else. You're jest all and everythink that heart could wish. It's all my own fault, Tudens; it's all my fault. You see, I git to thinkin' sometimes like I was a-goin' to *lose* you; and now that you are a-comin' on in years, and gittin' such a fine start, and all, and position and everythink.—Yes-sir! *position*, 'cause everybody likes you, Tudens. You know that; and I'm that proud of you and all, and that selfish, that it's onpossible I could ever, ever give you up;— never, never, *ever* give you up!" And Mr. Twiggs again stifled his voice in his handkerchief and blew his nose with prolonged violence.

It may have been the melancholy ticking of the clock, as it grated on the silence following, it may have been the gathering darkness of the room, or the plaintive sighing of the rising wind without, that caused the girl to shudder as she stooped to kiss the kind old face bent forward in the shadows, and turned with feigned gayety to the simple task of arranging supper. But when, a few minutes later, she announced that Twiggs and Tudens's tea was waiting, the two smilingly sat down, Mr. Twiggs remarking that if he only knew a blessing, he'd ask it upon that occasion most certainly.

"—For on'y look at these-'ere 'am and eggs," he said, admiringly: "I'd like to know if the Queen herself could cook 'em to a nicer turn, or serve 'em up more tantaliz'in'er to the palate. And this-'ere soup,—or whatever it is, is rich as gravy; and these boughten rolls ain't a bad thing either, split in two and toasted as you do 'em, air they, Tude?" And as Mr. Twiggs glanced inquiringly at his companion, he found her staring vacantly at her plate. "I was jest a-sayin', Tudens—" he went on, pretending to blow his tea and glancing cautiously across his saucer.

"Yes, Pop'm, I heard you;—we really *ought* to have a blessing, by all means."

Mr. Twiggs put down his tea without tasting it. "Tudens," he said, after a long pause, in which he carefully buttered a piece of toast for the second time,— "Tudens, I'm 'most afeard you didn't grasp that last remark of mine: I was a-sayin'—"

"Well—" said Tudens, attentively.

"I was a-sayin'," said Mr. Twiggs, averting his face and staring stoically at his toast—"I was a-sayin' that you was a-gittin' now to be quite a young woman."

"Oh, so you were," said Tudens, with charming naïveté.

"Well," said Mr. Twiggs, repentantly, but with a humorous twinkle, "if I wasn't a-sayin' of it, I was *a-thinkin'* it."—And then, running along hurriedly, "And I've been a-thinkin' it for days and days—ever sence you left the 'balley' and went in 'chambermaids,' and last in leadin' rôles. Maybe *you* ain't noticed it, but I've had my eyes on you from the 'flies' and the 'wings'; and jest betwixt us, Tudens, and not for me as ort to know better, and does know better, to go a-flatterin', at my time o'—or to go a-flatterin' anybody, as I said, after you're a-gittin' to be a young woman—and what's more, a werry *'andsome* young woman!"

"*Why, Pop'm!*" exclaimed Tudens, blushing.

"Yes, you are, Tudens, and I mean it, every word of it; and as I was a-goin' on to say, I've been a-watchin' of you, and a-layin' off a long time jest to tell you summat that will make your eyes open wider 'an that! What I mean," said Mr. Twiggs, coughing vehemently and pushing his chair back from the table—"what I mean is, you'll soon be old enough to be a-settin' up for yourself-like, and a-marry'—W'y, Tudens, what *ails* you?" The girl had risen to her feet, and, with a face dead white and lips all tremulous, stood clinging to her chair for support. "What ails you, Tudens?" repeated Mr. Twiggs, rising to his feet and gazing on her with a curious expression of alarm and tenderness.

"Nothing serious, dear Pop'm," said Tudens, with a flighty little laugh,—"only it just flashed on me all at once that I'd clean forgotten poor 'Dick's' supper." And as she turned abruptly to the parrot, cooing and clucking to him playfully,—up, up from some hitherto undreamed-of depth within the yearning heart of Mr. Twiggs mutely welled the old utterance, "Tude's a queer girl!"

"Whatever made you think of such a thing, Father?" called Tudens, gayly; and then, without waiting for an

"TWIGGS AND TUDENS"

answer, went on cooing to the parrot,—"Hey, old dicky-bird! do *you* think Tudens is a handsome young woman? and do *you* think Tudens is old enough to marry, eh?" This query delivered, she broke into a fit of merriment which so wrought upon the susceptibilities of the bird that he was heard repeatedly to declare and affirm, in most positive and unequivocal terms, that Tude had actually come home.

"Yes—*sir*, Tudens!" broke in Mr. Twiggs at last, lighting a fresh churchwarden and settling into his old position at the grate; "have your laugh out over it now, but it's a werry serious fact, for all that."

"I know it, Father," said the girl, recovering her gravity, turning her large eyes lovingly upon him and speaking very tenderly. "I know it—oh, I know it; and many, many times when I have thought of it, and then again of your old kindly faith; all the warm wealth of your love; and our old home here, and all the happiness it ever held for me and you alike—oh, I have tried hard—indeed, indeed I have—to put all other thought away and live for you alone! But, Pop'm! dear old Pop'm—" And even as the great strong breast made shelter for her own, the woman's heart within her flowed away in mists of gracious tears.

"Couldn't live without old Pop'm, could her?" half

cried and laughed the happy Mr. Twiggs, tangling his clumsy fingers in the long dark hair that fell across his arm, and bending till his glad face touched her own.—"Couldn't live without old Pop'm?"

"Never! never!" sobbed the girl, lifting her brimming eyes and gazing in the kind old face. "Oh, may I always live with you, Pop'm? Always?—Forever?—"

"—And a day!" said Mr. Twiggs, emphatically.

"Even after I'm—" and she hid her face again.

"Even after—*what*, Tudens?"

"After I'm—after I'm—married?" murmured Tudens, with a longing pressure.

"Nothink short!" said Mr. Twiggs;—"perwidin'," he added, releasing one hand and smoothing back his scanty hair—"perwidin', of course, that your man is a' honest, straitforrerd feller, as ain't no lordly notions nor nothink o' that sort."

"Nor rich?"

"Well, I ain't so p'ticklar about his bein' *pore*, adzackly. —Say a feller as works for his livin', and knows how to 'usband his earnin's thrifty-like, and allus 'as a hextry crown or two laid up against a rainy day—and a good perwider, of course," said Mr. Twiggs, with a comfortable glance around the room.—"'Ll blow me if I didn't see a face there a-peerin' in the winder!"

"TWIGGS AND TUDENS"

"Oh, no, you didn't," said the girl, without raising her head. "Go on—'and a good provider—'"

"—A good perwider," continued Mr. Twiggs; "and a feller, of course, as has a' eye out for the substantials of this life, and ain't afeard o' work—that's the idear! that's the idear!" said Mr. Twiggs, by way of sweeping conclusion.

"And that's all old Pop'm asks, after all?" queried the girl, with her radiant face wistful as his own.

"W'y, certainly!" said Mr. Twiggs, with heartiness. "Ain't that all and everythink to make home happy?"—catching her face between his great brown hands and kissing her triumphantly.

"Hooray for Twiggs-and Twiggs-and Twiggs-and—" cootered the drowsy bird, disjointedly.

The girl had risen.—"And you'll forgive me for marrying such a man?"

"Won't I?" said Mr. Twiggs, with a rapturous twinkle.

As he spoke, she flung her arms about his neck and pressed her lips close, close against his cheek, her own glad face now fronting the little window. . . . She heard the clicking of the latch, the opening of the door, and the step of the intruder ere she loosed her hold.

"God bless you, Pop'm, and forgive me!—This is my husband."

"TWIGGS AND TUDENS"

The newcomer, Mr. Stanley, reached and grasped the hand of Mr. Twiggs, eagerly, fervidly, albeit the face he looked on then will haunt him to the hour of his death.—Yet haply, some day, when the Master takes the selfsame hand within his own and whispers, "Tude's come home," the old smile will return.

DOLORES

LITHE-ARMED, and with satin-soft shoulders
   As white as the cream-crested wave;
With a gaze dazing every beholder's,
   She holds every gazer a slave:
Her hair, a fair haze, is outfloated
   And flared in the air like a flame;
Bare-breasted, bare-browed and bare-throated—
   Too smooth for the soothliest name.

She wiles you with wine, and wrings for you
   Ripe juices of citron and grape;
She lifts up her lute and sings for you
   Till the soul of you seeks no escape;
And you revel and reel with mad laughter,
   And fall at her feet, at her beck,
And the scar of her sandal thereafter
   You wear like a gyve round your neck.

WHEN I DO MOCK

When I do mock the blackness of the night
With my despair—outweep the very dews
And wash my wan cheeks stark of all delight,
Denying every counsel of dear use
In mine embittered state; with infinite
Perversity, mine eyes drink in no sight
Of pleasance that nor moon nor stars refuse
In silver largess and gold twinklings bright;—
I question me what mannered brain is mine
That it doth trick me of the very food
It panteth for—the very meat and wine
That yet should plump my starved soul with good
And comfortable plethora of ease,
That I might drowse away such rhymes as these.

MY MARY

My Mary, O my Mary!
   The simmer skies are blue:
The dawnin' brings the dazzle,
   An' the gloamin' brings the dew,—
The mirk o' nicht the glory
   O' the moon, an' kindles, too,
The stars that shift aboon the lift.—
   But naething brings me you!

Where is it, O my Mary,
   Ye are biding a' the while?
I ha' wended by your window—
   I ha' waited by the stile,
An' up an' down the river
   I ha' won for mony a mile,
Yet never found, adrift or drown'd,
   Your lang-belated smile.

MY MARY

Is it forgot, my Mary,
   How glad we used to be?—
The simmer-time when bonny bloomed
   The auld trysting-tree,—
How there I carved the name for you,
   An' you the name for me;
An' the gloamin' kenned it only
   When we kissed sae tenderly.

Speek ance to me, my Mary!—
   But whisper in my ear
As light as ony sleeper's breath,
   An' a' my soul will hear;
My heart shall stap its beating,
   An' the soughing atmosphere
Be hushed the while I leaning smile
   An' listen to you, dear!

My Mary, O my Mary!
   The blossoms bring the bees;
The sunshine brings the blossoms,
   An' the leaves on a' the trees;
The simmer brings the sunshine
   An' the fragrance o' the breeze,—

MY MARY

But O wi'out you, Mary,
　　I care naething for these!

We were sae happy, Mary!
　　O think how ance we said—
Wad ane o' us gae fickle,
　　Or ane o' us lie dead,—
To feel anither's kisses
　　We wad feign the auld instead,
An' ken the ither's footsteps
　　In the green grass owerhead.

My Mary, O my Mary!
　　Are ye dochter o' the air,
That ye vanish aye before me
　　As I follow everywhere?—
Or is it ye are only
　　But a mortal, wan wi' care,
Sin' I search through a' the kirkyird
　　An' I dinna find ye there?

EROS

The storm of love has burst at last
*   Full on me: All the world, before,*
*   Was like an alien, unknown shore*
Along whose verge I laughing passed.—
*   But now—I laugh not any more,—*
Bowed with a silence vast in weight
*   As that which falls on one who stands*
*   For the first time on ocean sands,*
Seeing and feeling all the great
*   Awe of the waves as they wash the lands*
And billow and wallow and undulate.

ORLIE WILDE

A GODDESS, with a siren's grace,—
A sun-haired girl on a craggy place
Above a bay where fish-boats lay
Drifting about like birds of prey.

Wrought was she of a painter's dream,—
Wise only as are artists wise,
My artist-friend, Rolf Herschkelhiem,
With deep sad eyes of oversize,
And face of melancholy guise.

I pressed him that he tell to me
This masterpiece's history.
He turned—*re*turned—and thus beguiled
Me with the tale of Orlie Wilde:—

"We artists live ideally:
We breed our firmest facts of air;
We make our own reality—

ORLIE WILDE

We dream a thing and it is so.
The fairest scenes we ever see
Are mirages of memory;
The sweetest thoughts we ever know
We plagiarize from Long Ago:
And as the girl on canvas there
Is marvellously rare and fair,
'Tis only inasmuch as she
Is dumb and may not speak to me!"
He tapped me with his mahlstick—then
The picture,—and went on again:

"Orlie Wilde, the fisher's child—
I see her yet, as fair and mild
As ever nursling summer day
Dreamed on the bosom of the bay:
For I was twenty then, and went
Alone and long-haired—all content
With promises of sounding name
And fantasies of future fame,
And thoughts that now my mind discards
As editor a fledgling bard's.

"At evening once I chanced to go,
With pencil and portfolio,

ORLIE WILDE

Adown the street of silver sand
That winds beneath this craggy land,
To make a sketch of some old scurf
Of driftage, nosing through the surf
A splintered mast, with knarl and strand
Of rigging-rope and tattered threads
Of flag and streamer and of sail
That fluttered idly in the gale
Or whipped themselves to sadder shreds.
The while I wrought, half listlessly,
On my dismantled subject, came
A sea-bird, settling on the same
With plaintive moan, as though that he
Had lost his mate upon the sea;
And—with my melancholy trend—
It brought dim dreams half understood—
It wrought upon my morbid mood,—
I thought of my own voyagings
That had no end—that have no end.—
And, like the sea-bird, I made moan
That I was loveless and alone.
And when at last with weary wings
It went upon its wanderings,
With upturned face I watched its flight
Until this picture met my sight:

ORLIE WILDE

A goddess, with a siren's grace, —
A sun-haired girl on a craggy place
Above a bay where fish-boats lay
Drifting about like birds of prey.

"In airy poise she, gazing, stood
A matchless form of womanhood,
That brought a thought that if for me
Such eyes had sought across the sea,
I could have swum the widest tide
That ever mariner defied,
And, at the shore, could on have gone
To that high crag she stood upon,
To there entreat and say, 'My Sweet,
Behold thy servant at thy feet.'
And to my soul I said: 'Above,
There stands the idol of thy love!'

"In this rapt, awed, ecstatic state
I gazed — till lo! I was aware
A fisherman had joined her there —
A weary man, with halting gait,
Who toiled beneath a basket's weight:
Her father, as I guessed, for she
Had run to meet him gleefully

ORLIE WILDE

And ta'en his burden to herself,
That perched upon her shoulder's shelf
So lightly that she, tripping, neared
A jutting crag and disappeared;
But left the echo of a song
That thrills me yet, and will as long
As I have being! . . .

    . . . "Evenings came
And went,—but each the same—the same:
She watched above, and even so
I stood there watching from below;
Till, grown so bold at last, I sung,—
(What matter now the theme thereof!)—
It brought an answer from her tongue—
Faint as the murmur of a dove,
Yet all the more the song of love. . . .

"I turned and looked upon the bay,
With palm to forehead—eyes a-blur
In the sea's smile—meant but for her!—
I saw the fish-boats far away
In misty distance, lightly drawn
In chalk-dots on the horizon—
Looked back at her, long, wistfully,—

And, pushing off an empty skiff,
I beckoned her to quit the cliff
And yield me her rare company
Upon a little pleasure-cruise.—
She stood, as loathful to refuse,
To muse for full a moment's time,—
Then answered back in pantomime
'She feared some danger from the sea
Were she discovered thus with me.'
I motioned then to ask her if
I might not join her on the cliff;
And back again, with graceful wave
Of lifted arm, she answer gave
'She feared some danger from the sea.'

"Impatient, piqued, impetuous, I
Sprang in the boat, and flung 'Good-bye'
From pouted mouth with angry hand,
And madly pulled away from land
With lusty stroke, despite that she
Held out her hands entreatingly:
And when far out, with covert eye
I shoreward glanced, I saw her fly
In reckless haste adown the crag,
Her hair a-flutter like a flag

ORLIE WILDE

Of gold that danced across the strand
In little mists of silver sand.
All curious I, pausing, tried
To fancy what it all implied,—
When suddenly I found my feet
Were wet; and, underneath the seat
On which I sat, I heard the sound
Of gurgling waters, and I found
The boat aleak alarmingly. . . .
I turned and looked upon the sea,
Whose every wave seemed mocking me;
I saw the fishers' sails once more—
In dimmer distance than before;
I saw the sea-bird wheeling by,
With foolish wish that *I* could fly:
I thought of firm earth, home and friends—
I thought of everything that tends
To drive a man to frenzy and
To wholly lose his own command;
I thought of all my waywardness—
Thought of a mother's deep distress;
Of youthful follies yet unpurged—
Sins, as the seas, about me surged—
Thought of the printer's ready pen
To-morrow drowning me again;—

ORLIE WILDE

A million things without a name—
I thought of everything but—Fame. . . .

"A memory yet is in my mind,
So keenly clear and sharp-defined,
I picture every phase and line
Of life and death, and neither mine,—
While some fair seraph, golden-haired,
Bends over me,—with white arms bared,
That strongly plait themselves about
My drowning weight and lift me out—
With joy too great for words to state
Or tongue to dare articulate!

"And this seraphic ocean-child
And heroine was Orlie Wilde:
And thus it was I came to hear
Her voice's music in my ear—
Ay, thus it was Fate paved the way
That I walk desolate to-day!" . . .

The artist paused and bowed his face
Within his palms a little space,
While reverently on his form
I bent my gaze and marked a storm

ORLIE WILDE

That shook his frame as wrathfully
As some typhoon of agony,
And fraught with sobs—the more profound
For that peculiar laughing sound
We hear when strong men weep. . . . I leant
With warmest sympathy—I bent
To stroke with soothing hand his brow,
He murmuring—"'Tis over now!—
And shall I tie the silken thread
Of my frail romance?" "Yes," I said.—
He faintly smiled; and then, with brow
In kneading palm, as one in dread—
His tasselled cap pushed from his head;—
"'Her voice's music,' I repeat,"
He said,—"'twas sweet—O passing sweet!—
Though she herself, in uttering
Its melody, proved not the thing
Of loveliness my dreams made meet
For me—there, yearning, at her feet—
Prone at her feet—a worshipper,—
For lo! she spake a tongue," moaned he,
"Unknown to me;—unknown to me
As mine to her—as mine to her."

LEONAINIE

LEONAINIE—Angels named her;
   And they took the light
Of the laughing stars and framed her
   In a smile of white;
      And they made her hair of gloomy
      Midnight, and her eyes of bloomy
      Moonshine, and they brought her to me
   In the solemn night.—

In a solemn night of summer,
   When my heart of gloom
Blossomed up to greet the comer
   Like a rose in bloom;
      All forebodings that distressed me
      I forgot as Joy caressed me—
      (*Lying* Joy! that caught and pressed me
   In the arms of doom!)

LEONAINIE

Only spake the little lisper
  In the Angel-tongue;
Yet I, listening, heard her whisper,—
  "Songs are only sung
    Here below that they may grieve you—
    Tales but told you to deceive you,—
    So must Leonainie leave you
  While her love is young."

Then God smiled and it was morning.
  Matchless and supreme
Heaven's glory seemed adorning
  Earth with its esteem:
    Every heart but mine seemed gifted
    With the voice of prayer, and lifted
    Where my Leonainie drifted
  From me like a dream.

TO A JILTED SWAIN

Get thee back neglected friends;
And repay, as each one lends,
Tithes of shallow-sounding glee
Or keen-ringing raillery:
Get thee from lone vigils; be
But in jocund company,
Where is laughter and acclaim
Boisterous above the name.—
Get where sulking husbands sip
Ale-house cheer, with pipe at lip;
And where Mol the barmaid saith
Curst is she that marrieth.

THE VOICES

Down in the night I hear them:
    The Voices—unknown—unguessed,—
That whisper, and lisp, and murmur,
    And will not let me rest.—

Voices that seem to question,
    In unknown words, of me,
Of fabulous ventures, and hopes and dreams
    Of this and the World to be.

Voices of mirth and music,
    As in sumptuous homes; and sounds
Of mourning, as of gathering friends
    In country burial-grounds.

Cadence of maiden voices—
    Their lovers' blent with these;

THE VOICES

And of little children singing,
   As under orchard trees.

And often, up from the chaos
   Of my deepest dreams, I hear
Sounds of their phantom laughter
   Filling the atmosphere:

They call to me from the darkness;
   They cry to me from the gloom,
Till I start sometimes from my pillow
   And peer through the haunted room;

When the face of the moon at the window
   Wears a pallor like my own,
And seems to be listening with me
   To the low, mysterious tone,—

The low, mysterious clamor
   Of voices that seem to be
Striving in vain to whisper
   Of secret things to me;—

Of a something dread to be warned of;
   Of a rapture yet withheld;

THE VOICES

Or hints of the marvellous beauty
   Of songs unsyllabled.

But ever and ever the meaning
   Falters and fails and dies,
And only the silence quavers
   With the sorrow of my sighs.

And I answer:—O Voices, ye may not
   Make me to understand
Till my own voice, mingling with you,
   Laughs in the Shadow-land.

A BAREFOOT BOY

A barefoot boy! I mark him at his play—
  For May is here once more, and so is he,—
  His dusty trousers, rolled half to the knee,
And his bare ankles grimy, too, as they:
Cross-hatchings of the nettle, in array
  Of feverish stripes, hint vividly to me
  Of woody pathways winding endlessly
Along the creek, where even yesterday
He plunged his shrinking body—gasped and shook—
  Yet called the water "warm," with never lack
Of joy. And so, half enviously I look
  Upon this graceless barefoot and his track,—
  His toe stubbed—ay, his big toe-nail knocked back
Like unto the clasp of an old pocket-book.

THE YOUTHFUL PATRIOT

O WHAT did the little boy do
'At nobody wanted him to?
Didn't do nothin' but romp an' run,
An' whoop an' holler an' bang his gun
An' bu'st fire-crackers, an' ist have fun—
    An' '*at's* all the little boy done!

PONCHUS PILUT

PONCHUS PILUT *ust* to be
Ist a *Slave,* an' now he's *free.*
Slaves wuz on'y ist before
The War wuz—an' *ain't* no more.

He works on our place fer us,—
An' comes here—*sometimes* he does.
He shocks corn an' shucks it.—An'
He makes hominy "by han'!"—

Wunst he bringed us some, one trip,
Tied up in a piller-slip:
Pa says, when Ma cooked it, "MY!
This-here's gooder'n you *buy!*"

Ponchus *pats* fer me an' sings;
An' he says most *funny* things!
Ponchus calls a dish a "*deesh*"—
Yes, an' *he* calls fishes "*feesh*"!

PONCHUS PILUT

When Ma want him eat wiv us
He says, "'Skuse me—'deed you mus'!—
Ponchus know' good manners, Miss.—
He ain' eat wher' White-folks is!"

'Lindy takes *his* dinner out
Wher' he's workin'—roun' about.—
Wunst he et his dinner spread
In our ole wheelborry-bed.

Ponchus Pilut says "*'at's* not
His *right* name,—an' done fergot
What his *sho'-'nuff* name is now—
An' don' matter none *no*how!"

Yes, an' Ponchus he'ps Pa, too,
When our *butcherin's* to do,
An' scalds hogs—an' says, "Take care
'Bout it, er you'll *set the hair!*"

Yes, an' out in our back-yard
He he'ps 'Lindy rendur lard;
An', wite in the fire there, he
Roast' a pigtail wunst fer me.—

PONCHUS PILUT

An' ist nen th'ole tavurn-bell
Rung, down-town, an' he says, "Well!—
Hear dat! *Lan' o' Caanan*, Son,
Ain't dat bell say '*Pigtail done!*'

—'Pigtail done!
Go call Son!—
Tell dat
Chile dat
Pigtail done!'"[20]

A TWINTORETTE

Ho! my little maiden
    With the glossy tresses,
  Come thou and dance with me
    A measure all divine;
Let my breast be laden
    With but thy caresses—
Come thou and glancingly
    Mate thy face with mine.

Thou shalt trill a rondel,
    While my lips are purling
Some dainty twitterings
    Sweeter than the birds';
And, with arms that fondle
    Each as we go twirling,
We will kiss, with titterings,
    Lisps and loving words.

SLUMBER-SONG

SLEEP, little one! The Twilight folds her gloom
    Full tenderly about the drowsy Day,
And all his tinselled hours of light and bloom
        Like toys are laid away.

Sleep! sleep! The noon-sky's airy cloud of white
    Has deepened wide o'er all the azure plain;
And, trailing through the leaves, the skirts of Night
        Are wet with dews as rain.

But rest thou sweetly, smiling in thy dreams,
    With round fists tossed like roses o'er thy head,
And thy tranc'd lips and eyelids kissed with gleams
        Of rapture perfected.

THE CIRCUS PARADE

The Circus!—The Circus!—The throb of the drums,
And the blare of the horns, as the Band-wagon comes;
The clash and the clang of the cymbals that beat,
As the glittering pageant winds down the long street!

In the Circus parade there is glory clean down
From the first spangled horse to the mule of the Clown,
With the gleam and the glint and the glamour and glare
Of the days of enchantment all glimmering there!

And there are the banners of silvery fold
Caressing the winds with their fringes of gold,
And their high-lifted standards, with spear-tips aglow,
And the helmeted knights that go riding below.

There's the Chariot, wrought of some marvellous shell
The Sea gave to Neptune, first washing it well
With its fabulous waters of gold, till it gleams
Like the galleon rare of an Argonaut's dreams.

THE CIRCUS PARADE

And the Elephant, too, (with his undulant stride
That rocks the high throne of a king in his pride,)
That in jungles of India shook from his flanks
The tigers that leapt from the Jujubee-banks.

Here's the long, ever-changing, mysterious line
Of the Cages, with hints of their glories divine
From the barred little windows, cut high in the rear,
Where the close-hidden animals' noses appear.

Here's the Pyramid-car, with its splendor and flash,
And the Goddess on high, in a hot-scarlet sash
And a pen-wiper skirt!—O the rarest of sights
Is this "Queen of the Air" in cerulean tights!

Then the far-away clash of the cymbals, and then
The swoon of the tune ere it wakens again
With the capering tones of the gallant cornet
That go dancing away in a mad minuet.

The Circus!—The Circus!—The throb of the drums,
And the blare of the horns, as the Band-wagon comes;
The clash and the clang of the cymbals that beat,
As the glittering pageant winds down the long street.

FOLKS AT LONESOMEVILLE

Pore-folks lives at Lonesomeville—
  Lawzy! but they're pore!
Houses with no winders in,
  And hardly any door:
Chimbly all tore down, and no
  Smoke in that at all—
Ist a stovepipe through a hole
  In the kitchen-wall!

Pump 'at's got no handle on;
  And no woodshed—And, *wooh!*—
Mighty cold there, choppin' wood,
  Like pore-folks has to do!—
Winter-time, and snow and sleet
  Ist fairly fit to kill!—
Hope to goodness *Santy Claus*
  Goes to Lonesomeville!

THE THREE JOLLY HUNTERS

O THERE were three jolly hunters;
   And a-hunting they did go,
With a spaniel-dog, and a pointer-dog,
   And a setter-dog also.
                Looky there!

And they hunted and they hal-looed;
   And the first thing they did find
Was a dingling-dangling hornet's-nest
   A-swinging in the wind.
                Looky there!

And the first one said—"What is it?"
   Said the next, "We'll punch and see":
And the next one said, a mile from there,
   "I wish we'd let it be!"
                Looky there!

THE THREE JOLLY HUNTERS

And they hunted and they hal-looed;
   And the next thing they did raise
Was a bobbin' bunny cottontail
   That vanished from their gaze.
               Looky there!

One said it was a hot base-ball,
   Zipped through the brambly thatch,
But the others said 'twas a note by post,
   Or a telegraph-dispatch.
               Looky there!

So they hunted and they hal-looed;
   And the next thing they did sight
Was a great big bulldog chasing them,
   And a farmer, hollerin' "Skite!"
               Looky there!

And the first one said, "Hi-jinktum!"
   And the next, "Hi-jinktum-jee!"
And the last one said, "Them very words
   Had just occurred to me!"
               Looky there!

THE LITTLE DOG-WOGGY

A LITTLE Dog-Woggy
Once walked round the World:
So he shut up his house; and, forgetting
His two puppy-children
Locked in there, he curled
Up his tail in pink bombazine netting,
And set out
To walk round
The World.

He walked to Chicago,
And heard of the Fair—
Walked on to New York, where he *never*,—
In fact, he discovered
That many folks there
Thought less of Chicago than ever,
As he musing-
Ly walked round
The World.

THE LITTLE DOG-WOGGY

He walked on to Boston,
And round Bunker Hill,
Bow-wowed, but no citizen heerd him—
Till he ordered his baggage
And called for his bill,
And then, bless their souls! how they cheered him,
As he gladly
Walked on round
The World.

He walked and walked on
For a year and a day—
Dropped down at his own door and panted,
Till a teamster came driving
Along the highway
And told him that house there was ha'nted
By the two starve-
Dest pups in
The World.

CHARMS

I

FOR CORNS AND THINGS

Prune your corn in the gray of the morn
   With a blade that's shaved the dead,
And barefoot go and hide it so
   The rain will rust it red:
Dip your foot in the dew and put
   A print of it on the floor,
And stew the fat of a brindle cat,
   And say this o'er and o'er:—
      Corny! morny! blady! dead!
      Gory! sory! rusty! red!
      Footsy! putsy! floory! stew!
      Fatsy! catsy!
          Mew!
          Mew!
   Come grease my corn
     In the gray of the morn!
    Mew! Mew! Mew!

CHARMS

II

TO REMOVE FRECKLES—SCOTCH ONES

Gae the mirkest night an' stan'
'Twixt twa graves, ane either han';
Wi' the right han' fumblin' ken
Wha the deid mon's name's ance be'n,—
Wi' the ither han' sae read
Wha's neist neebor o' the deid;
An it be or wife or lass,
Smoor tha twa han's i' the grass,
Weshin' either wi' the ither,
Then tha faice wi' baith thegither;
Syne ye'll seeket at cockcraw—
Ilka freeckle's gang awa!

A FEW OF THE BIRD-FAMILY

THE Old Bob-white, and Chipbird;
   The Flicker, and Chewink,
And little hopty-skip bird
   Along the river-brink.

The Blackbird, and Snowbird,
   The Chicken-hawk, and Crane;
The glossy old black Crow-bird,
   And Buzzard down the lane.

The Yellowbird, and Redbird,
   The Tomtit, and the Cat;
The Thrush, and that Red*head*-bird
   The rest's all pickin' at!

The Jay-bird, and the Bluebird,
   The Sapsuck, and the Wren—
The Cockadoodle-doo-bird,
   And our old Settin'-hen!

THROUGH SLEEPY-LAND

W<small>HERE</small> do you go when you go to sleep,
   Little Boy! Little Boy! where?
'Way—'way in where's Little Bo-Peep,
And Little Boy Blue, and the Cows and Sheep
    A-wandering 'way in there—in there—
      A-wandering 'way in there!

And what do you see when lost in dreams,
   Little Boy, 'way in there?
Firefly-glimmers and glow-worm gleams,
And silvery, low, slow-sliding streams,
    And mermaids, smiling out—'way in where
      They're a-hiding—'way in there!

Where do you go when the Fairies call,
   Little Boy! Little Boy! where?
Wade through the dews of the grasses tall,
Hearing the weir and the waterfall
    And the Wee Folk—'way in there—in there—
      And the Kelpies—'way in there!

THROUGH SLEEPY-LAND

And what do you do when you wake at dawn,
   Little Boy! Little Boy! what?
Hug my Mommy and kiss her on
Her smiling eyelids, sweet and wan,
   And tell her everything I've forgot,
     A-wandering 'way in there—in there—
       Through the blind-world 'way in there!

THE TRESTLE AND THE BUCK-SAW

The Trestle and the Buck-Saw
   Went out a-walking once,
And staid away and staid away
   For days and weeks and months:
And when they got back home again,
   Of all that had occurred,
The neighbors said the gossips said
   They never said a word.

THE KING OF OO-RINKTUM-JING

DAINTY Baby Austin!
Your Daddy's gone to Boston
   To see the King
   Of Oo-Rinktum-Jing
And the whale he rode acrost on!

Boston Town's a city:
But O it's such a pity!—
   They'll greet the King
   Of Oo-Rinktum-Jing
With never a nursery ditty!

But me and you and Mother
Can stay with Baby-brother,
   And sing of the King
   Of Oo-Rinktum-Jing
And laugh at one another!

THE KING OF OO-RINKTUM-JING

  So what cares Baby Austin
If Daddy *has* gone to Boston
  To see the King
  Of Oo-Rinktum-Jing
And the whale he rode acrost on?

THE TOY PENNY-DOG

MA put my Penny-Dog
  Safe on the shelf,
An' left no one home but him,
  Me an' myself;
So I clumbed a big chair
  I pushed to the wall—
But the Toy Penny-Dog
  Ain't there at all!
I went back to Dolly—
  An' *she* 'uz gone too,
An' little Switch 'uz layin' there;—
  An' Ma says "*Boo!*"—
An' there she wuz a-peepin'
  Through the front-room door:
An' I ain't goin' to be a bad
  Little girl no more!

JARGON-JINGLE

TAWDERY!—faddery! Feathers and fuss!
Mummery!—flummery! wusser and wuss!
All o' Humanity—Vanity Fair!—
Heaven for nothin', and—nobody there!

THE GREAT EXPLORER

He sailed o'er the weltery watery miles
   For a tabular year-and-a-day,
To the kindless, kinkable Cannibal Isles
   He sailed and he sailed away!
He captured a loon in a wild lagoon,
   And a yak that weeps and smiles,
And a bustard-bird, and a blue baboon,
   In the kindless Cannibal Isles
     And wilds
       Of the kinkable Cannibal Isles.

He swiped in bats with his butterfly-net,
   In the kinkable Cannibal Isles,
And got short-waisted and over-het
   In the haunts of the crocodiles;
And nine or ten little Pygmy Men
   Of the quaintest shapes and styles
He shipped back home to his old Aunt Jenn,
   From the kindless Cannibal Isles
     And wilds
       Of the kinkable Cannibal Isles.

THE SCHOOL-BOY'S FAVORITE

" Over the river and through the wood
  Now Grandmother's cap I spy:
 Hurrah for the fun!—Is the pudding done?
  Hurrah for the pumpkin-pie!"
              SCHOOL READER.

FER any boy 'at's little as me,
  Er any little girl,
That-un's the goodest poetry-piece
  In any book in the worl'!
An' ef grown-peoples wuz little ag'in
  I bet they'd say so, too,
Ef *they'd* go see *their* ole Gran'ma,
  Like our Pa lets *us* do!

Over the river an' through the wood
  Now Gran'mother's cap I spy:
Hurrah fer the fun!—Is the puddin' done?—
  Hurrah fer the punkin-pie!

An' 'll tell you *why* 'at's the goodest piece:—
'Cause it's ist like *we* go
To *our* Gran'ma's, a-visitun there,
When our Pa he says so;
An Ma she fixes my little cape-coat
An' little fuzz-cap; an' Pa
He tucks me away—an' yells "*Hoo-ray!*"—
An' whacks Ole Gray, an' drives the sleigh
Fastest you ever saw!

Over the river an' through the wood
   Now Gran'mother's cap I spy:
Hurrah fer the fun!—Is the puddin' done?—
   Hurrah fer the punkin-pie!

An' Pa ist snuggles me 'tween his knees—
An' I he'p hold the lines,
An' peek out over the buffalo-robe;—
An' the wind ist *blows!*—an' the snow ist *snows!*—
An' the sun ist shines! an' shines!—
An th' ole horse tosses his head an' coughs
The frost back in our face.—
An' I' ruther go to my Gran'ma's
Than any other place!

THE SCHOOL-BOY'S FAVORITE

Over the river an' through the wood
  Now Gran'mother's cap I spy:
Hurrah fer the fun!—Is the puddin' done?—
  Hurrah fer the punkin-pie!

An' all the peoples they is in town
  Watches us whizzin' past
To go a-visitun *our* Gran'ma's,
  Like we all went there last;—
But *they* can't go, like ist *our* folks
  An' Johnny an' Lotty, an' three
Er four neighber-childerns, an' Rober-ut Volney,
  An' Charley an' Maggy an' me!

Over the river an' through the wood
  Now Gran'mother's cap I spy:
Hurrah fer the fun!—Is the puddin' done?—
  Hurrah fer the punkin-pie!

ALBUMANIA

Some certain misty yet tenable signs
  Of the oracular Raggedy Man,
Happily found in these fugitive lines
  Culled from the album of 'Lizabuth Ann.

FRIENDSHIP

O FRIENDSHIP, when I muse on you,
As thoughtful minds, O Friendship, do,
I muse, O Friendship, o'er and o'er,
O Friendship—as I said before.

LIFE

"What is Life?" If the *Dead* might say,
  'Spect they'd answer, under breath,
Sorry-like yet a-laughin':—A
  Poor pale yesterday of Death!

ALBUMANIA

LIFE'S HAPPIEST HOURS

Best, I guess,
    Was the old "*Recess.*"—
'Way back there's where I'd love to be—
    Shet of each lesson and hateful rule,
When the whole round World was as sweet to me
    As the big ripe apple I brung to School.

MARION-COUNTY MAN HOMESICK ABROAD

I, who had hobnobbed with the shades of kings,
    And canvassed grasses from old masters' graves,
And in cathedrals stood and looked at things
    In niches, crypts and naves;—
My heavy heart was sagging with its woe,
    Nor Hope to prop it up, nor Promise, nor
One woman's hands—and O I wanted so
    To be felt sorry for!

BIRDY! BIRDY!

The Redbreast loves the blooming bough—
    The Bluebird loves it same as he;—

ALBUMANIA

And as they sit and sing there now,
  So do I sing to thee—
Only, dear heart, unlike the birds,
  I do not climb a tree
    To sing—
  I do not climb a tree.

When o'er this page, in happy years to come,
  Thou jokest on these lines and on my name,
Doubt not my love and say, "Though he lies dumb,
  He's lying, just the same!"

THE LITTLE MOCK-MAN

THE Little Mock-man on the Stairs—
He mocks the lady's horse 'at rares
   At bi-sickles an' things,—
He mocks the mens 'at rides 'em, too;
An' mocks the Movers, drivin' through,
An' hollers, "Here's the way *you* do
   With them-air hitchin'-strings!"
   "Ho! ho!" he'll say,
   Ole Settlers' Day,
   When they're all jogglin' by,—
   "You look like *this*,"
   He'll say, an' twis'
His mouth an' squint his eye
An' 'tend-like *he* wuz beat the bass
   Drum at both ends—an' toots an' blares
Ole dinner-horn an' puffs his face—
   The Little Mock-man on the Stairs!

THE LITTLE MOCK-MAN

The Little Mock-man on the Stairs
Mocks all the peoples all he cares
   'At passes up an' down!
He mocks the chickens round the door,
An' mocks the girl 'at scrubs the floor,
An' mocks the rich, an' mocks the pore,
   An' ever'thing in town!
   "Ho! ho!" says he,
     To you er me;
   An' ef we turns an' looks,
     He's all cross-eyed
     An' mouth all wide
   Like Giunts is, in books.—
"Ho! ho!" he yells, "look here at *me*,"
An' rolls his fat eyes roun' an' glares,—
"*You* look like *this!*" he says, says he—
The Little Mock-man on the Stairs!

The Little Mock—
  The Little Mock—
    The Little Mock-man on the Stairs,
He mocks the music-box an' clock,
  An' roller-sofy an' the chairs;
He mocks his Pa, an' specs he wears;
He mocks the man 'at picks the pears

THE LITTLE MOCK-MAN

An' plums an' peaches on the shares;
He mocks the monkeys an' the bears
On picture-bills, an' rips an' tears
'Em down,—an' mocks ist all he cares,
An' EVER'body EVER'wheres!

SUMMER-TIME AND WINTER-TIME

In the golden noon-shine,
   Or in the pink of dawn;
In the silver moonshine,
   Or when the moon is gone;
Open eyes, or drowsy lids,
   'Wake or 'most asleep,
I can hear the katydids,—
   "Cheep! Cheep! Cheep!"

Only in the winter-time
   Do they ever stop,
In the chip-and-splinter-time,
   When the backlogs pop,—
Then it is, the kettle-lids,
   While the sparkles leap,
Lisp like the katydids,—
   "Cheep! Cheep! Cheep!"

HOME-MADE RIDDLES—

ALL BUT THE ANSWERS

I

No one ever saw it
   Till I dug it from the ground;
I found it when I lost it,
   And lost it when I found:
I washed it, and dressed it,
   And buried it once more—
Dug it up, and loved it then
   Better than before.
I was paid for finding it—
   I don't know why or how,—
But I lost, found, and kept it,
   And haven't got it now.

II

Sometimes it's all alone—
 Sometimes in a crowd;
It says a thousand bright things,
 But never talks aloud.
Everybody loves it,
 And likes to have it call.
But if you shouldn't happen to,
 It wouldn't care at all.
First you see or hear of it,
 It's a-singing,—then
You may look and listen,
 But it never sings again.

THE LOVELY CHILD

Lilies are both pure and fair,
Growing 'midst the roses there—
Roses, too, both red and pink,
Are quite beautiful, I think.

But of all bright blossoms—best—
Purest—fairest—loveliest,—
Could there be a sweeter thing
Than a primrose, blossoming?

THE YELLOWBIRD

Hey! my little Yellowbird,
  What you doing there?
Like a flashing sun-ray,
  Flitting everywhere:
Dangling down the tall weeds
  And the hollyhocks,
And the lordly sunflowers
  Along the garden-walks.

Ho! my gallant Golden-bill,
  Pecking 'mongst the weeds,
You must have for breakfast
  Golden flower-seeds:
Won't you tell a little fellow
  What you have for *tea?*—
'Spect a peck o' yellow, mellow
  Pippin on the tree.

ENVOY

When but a little boy, it seemed
   My dearest rapture ran
In fancy ever, when I dreamed
   I was a man—a man!

Now—sad perversity!—my theme
   Of rarest, purest joy
Is when, in fancy blest, I dream
   I am a little boy.